# DATE DUE

| | | | |
|---|---|---|---|
| NO 21 '97 | | | |
| RENEW | | | |
| OE 16 '07 | | | |
| JE 18 '99 | | | |
| | | | |
| MY 25 '00 | | | |
| DE 2 0 00 | | | |
| | | | |
| | | | |
| AP 28 '04 | | | |
| | | | |
| | | | |
| | | | |
| | | | |
| | | | |
| | | | |
| | | | |

# BALANCING THE FEDERAL BUDGET

Edited by J. W. AROS

## THE REFERENCE SHELF

Volume 68 Number 2

THE H. W. WILSON COMPANY

New York   Dublin   1996

ELF

Balancing the federal budget

articles, excerpts from
s of social trends in the
numbers to a volume, all
ıdar year. Numbers one
t, give background infor-
view, concluding with a
comprehensive bibliography that contains books, pamphlets and abstracts
of additional articles on the subject. The final number is a collection of
recent speeches. This number also contains a subject index to the entire
Reference Shelf volume. Books in the series may be purchased individu-
ally or on subscription.

**Library of Congress Cataloging-in-Publication Data**

Balancing the federal budget / edited by J. W. Aros.
    p.   cm.—(The reference shelf ; v. 68, no. 2)
    Includes bibliographical references.
    ISBN 0-8242-0887-0
    1. Budget deficits—United States.   2. Deficit financing—United
States.   I. Aros, J. W. II.   Series
HJ2051.B26   1996
336.3′0973—dc20                                        96-6130
                                                        CIP

*Cover:* Treasury Department personnel look over U.S. government budget appendixes. *Photo:* Bettmann Newsphotos

Printed in the United States of America

# CONTENTS

III.  CUTTING ENTITLEMENTS

IV.  FINDING THE WILL

# PREFACE

On November 13, 1995 most operations of the United States government were forced to shut down for a period of six days. Offices were closed and employees were sent home for the duration. Operations resumed but were closed again on December 16, 1995, this time for 21 days, the longest government shutdown in U.S. history. Both shutdowns—and the possibility of others still to come—were the result of the inability of Congress, particularly the House of Representatives with its Contract with America, and the President to agree on a federal budget for the 1996 fiscal year, which had commenced on October 1, 1995.

A federal budget contains the funding to run the government's operations for an entire fiscal year. In most years the budget is approved before the new fiscal year begins. When Congress and the President do not agree on a budget before a new fiscal year has started, the government is technically out of money to pay its employees, run its programs, and meet its other financial obligations. To avoid a shutdown, Congress usually passes a temporary funding measure to keep the government going while the budget discussions continue.

In the fall of 1995, however, the Congress—dominated by the Republicans for the first time in many years—and the President, a Democrat, had such different ideas of how much money the federal government should spend in the new fiscal year—and on which programs—that the process of reaching agreement was slowed down to the point of gridlock. Moreover, many senators and representatives wished to begin the process of achieving a *balanced* federal budget—i.e., a situation in which federal spending does not exceed the sum of taxes the government would take in—so that when the President and the Congress failed to reach a compromise, the Congress, in order to put pressure on the President, refused to authorize the temporary spending measures that would keep the government going. This is what forced the U.S. government to shutdown twice.

As this compilation was being put together, short-term funding legislation had been passed to end each of the shutdowns, but no overall budget agreement reached. What was preventing the parties from reaching an agreement? Politics, of course, is one obvious reason: 1996 is a presidential election year. Beyond politics, there is a philosophical disagreement over how big a government the nation should have. Then there are differences of opinion over which government programs should be funded and at what level and which should be cut. Behind all these arguments, however, lies the issue of whether the country should, or even could, have a balanced budget. The debate over how to reach a balanced budget, how long it would take to achieve, and how much sacrifice would be required by the nation's citizens was the real cause of the two shutdowns.

When the federal government spends more than it takes in that same year, the result is a budget deficit. In order to meet the deficit—i.e., to raise the extra funds—the government has to borrow money by issuing bonds, which investors buy and which the government is obliged to pay back with interest on a fixed schedule. Sometimes a government faces situations that require it to borrow money—when war breaks out, for example—but critics of deficit financing say that government borrowing ought to be reserved for emergencies and should be followed quickly by raised taxes or reduced spending. To fund its wide range of operations and programs, which include defense, social security, Medicare, welfare, agricultural price supports, foreign aid, and much more, the U.S. government has been running deficits for many years—every year but four since 1954—and borrowing the money to cover them. While the deficit in the 1995 fiscal year was $192 million, a smaller deficit than in any of the last few years, if you add it to all the deficits from previous years that have not been paid off, you arrive at the total national debt, which by the end of 1995 had reached $4.9 trillion. Given the size of the debt, it is not surprising that one of the largest expense items in recent budgets has been the interest payments on the national debt, which by themselves sometimes equal or even exceed the size of the annual deficits.

This Reference Shelf compilation offers a wide range of opinions on the subjects of federal deficits, the national debt, and a balanced budget, as well as the budget's impact on the nation's economy and on social programs like Medicare and welfare. The articles in Section One, "Deficits and the National Debt," discuss the history of budget deficits and describe some of the attempts to eliminate them.

Section Two, "A Constitutional Amendment," explores the viability of a device to force future administrations and congresses not to overspend: a balanced budget amendment to the United States constitution.

Throughout all the debates and harangues on the subject of a balanced budget, one word is continually heard, "entitlements." The articles in Section Three, "Cutting Entitlements," discuss those social programs whose annual expenditures, if they are not trimmed, most likely threaten the prospect of ever achieving a balanced budget: social security, Medicare, and Medicaid.

Section Four, "Finding the Will," deals primarily with whether there are other ways to cut the budget that are more feasible and less contentious than slashing entitlements and whether Congress has the political will to find them.

The editor wishes to thank the authors and publishers who kindly granted permission to reprint the material in this collection.

J. W. Aros

December 1995

# I. DEFICITS AND THE NATIONAL DEBT

## EDITOR'S INTRODUCTION

For many people the national debt fails to become more than a very large number, with little meaning. Who owes this 4.9 trillion dollar debt to whom? How long has this money been owed? How can it be paid off?

The history of the national debt, or the total amount of money owed by the government, is told by John Steele Gordon in "The Federal Debt." Gordon traces the economic patterns of the federal government from 1792 to the present and relates them to historical events that have led either to surpluses or deficits. Gordon notes that for most of its history, the federal government operated on a pay-as-you-go basis, which until 1930 produced twice as many annual budget surpluses as deficits. In 1930 came the Great Depression, followed by the Roosevelt administrations' New Deal spending programs which were blessed by the Keynesian economic doctrine that a government could and should pursue an active role in affecting the nation's supply and demand through its taxing and spending policies. Since 1931 there have been budget deficits in 46 of the 54 years.

George Marotta discusses his fears of the future in his speech, "How to Shrink the U.S. Budget Deficit." Using a variety of statistics, he examines the deficit and national debt from a number of angles: one statistic is that each person—including children and retired persons—is in debt by $18,846 as soon as they are born. The principal culprits, in his opinion, are the American public, elected officials, and the bureaucrats. He concludes that Congress does not really want to balance the budget but instead prefers just to control spending.

The true cause of the deficits has long been debated. Some, like former Secretary of the Treasury Lloyd Bentsen, in an article entitled "Why the Deficit?", asserts that it is simply overspending during the 1980s that must be faced. Taking a different tack, a leading economist, author and professor of economics Robert Eisner, writing in *The New York Times*, argues that the national debt is not a threatening reality but an asset of the American people who as individuals will bequeath the asset to their children.

Frank Lalli, the managing editor of *Money*, turns to the hard numbers in an article called "How to Balance the Budget—for Real." He provides an objective analysis of what the government spends and what would have to be cut if a balanced budget is to become reality.

The final article is a *Challenge* magazine interview with Robert Reischauer, former Director of Congressional Budget Office (CBO). Reischauer discusses the recent history of the deficits and the various plans for their elimination. He points out that to date the government has managed to resolve about half of the underlying budget problems that faced the country during 1990.

---

## THE FEDERAL DEBT[1]

---

The federal government was still in the process of establishing itself in 1792 and did not have a good year financially. Total income was only $3,670,000, or 88 cents per capita. Outlays were $5,080,000. The budget deficit therefore amounted to fully 38 percent of revenues. The next year, however, the government sharply reduced expenses while enjoying increased tax receipts and showed its first budget surplus. Except during periods of grave economic or military crisis, the government would never again run up so large an annual deficit in terms of a percentage of total revenues.

Not, that is, until the peaceful and relatively prosperous year of 1992. That year the federal government had revenues of $1.076 trillion and outlays of $1.475 trillion, a budget deficit equaling 37 percent of revenues. Everyone, conservative and liberal alike, agrees that something is terribly wrong with how the United States government conducts its fiscal affairs today. The last eighteen years of the nation's history have been marked by a more than 25 percent increase in federal revenues (in constant dollars) and the collapse of our only significant external military

[1]Article by John Steel Gordon from *American Heritage* 46:82–92 N '95. Copyright © Forbes, Inc., 1995. Reprinted with permission of AMERICAN HERITAGE Magazine, a division of Forbes, Inc.

threat. Yet in those years the United States has spent as much of tomorrow's money as we would have spent fighting a major war or new Great Depression. That will have no small consequences if tomorrow we actually have to fight one.

How did the world's oldest continuously constituted republic lose control of so fundamental a responsibility as its own budget? The answer is, as with most governmental policy disasters in a democracy, one innocuous step at a time. While politicians, economists, and many others pursued their self-interests, the national interest largely got lost in the shuffle.

Over the last sixty years five trends have increasingly affected government fiscal policy. First, a powerful but fundamentally flawed concept in the discipline of economics has completely changed the way both economists and politicians view the national economy and their responsibilities toward it. Second, the responsibilities of government in general and the federal government in particular, as viewed by the public, have greatly increased. Third, a shift in power from the Executive to Congress has balkanized the budget process by sharply limiting the influence of the one politician in Washington whose constituency is national in scope, the President. Fourth, the decay of party discipline and the seniority system within Congress itself has further balkanized the budget process, dividing it among innumerable committees and subcommittees. This has made logrolling (you vote for my program and I'll vote for yours) the order of the day on Capitol Hill. Finally, the political-action-committee system of financing congressional elections has given greatly increased influence to spending constituencies (often called special interests, especially when they are funding someone else's campaign) while sharply reducing that of the electorate as a whole, which picks up the tab.

The result is a budget system that has become ever more heavily biased toward spending. As a consequence, the national debt has been spiraling upward, first only in absolute numbers and then, in the last twelve years, as a percentage of the gross national product as well. Today it stands at about 68 percent of the annual GNP [Gross National Product], higher than it has ever been in peacetime except in the immediate aftermath of a great war.

To be sure, a country as rich and productive as the United States can well afford to service its present debt. But the current trend is ominous, to put it mildly. Just consider: In the first 204 years of our independence, we took on the burden of a trillion dollars of debt, mostly to fight the wars that made and preserved us a nation. In the last fifteen, however, we have taken on four trillion more for no better reason, when it comes right down to it, than to spare a few hundred people in Washington the political inconvenience of having to say no to one constituent or another.

### Adam Smith's Good Housekeeping

The new United States emerged from the Revolution sovereign but in a state of fiscal chaos. The Continental Congress had been forced to resort to printing fiat money, the so-called continentals that sank quickly into worthlessness. The various states had borrowed heavily to meet the demands of the war.

The central government under the Articles of Confederation was financed solely by contributions from the various state governments (just as the United Nations is funded today) and had no power to tax or borrow on its own authority. Because the state governments had pressing needs of their own (as governments always do), their contributions were often late and sometimes nonexistent. As a result, the central government had grave difficulties meeting even its current obligations.

It was this financial crisis that helped force the drafting of the new Constitution in 1787. The document that the Founding Fathers created that summer in Philadelphia—the desperate poverty of the old government all too fresh in their minds—put remarkably few restrictions on the new government's power to spend, tax, and borrow.

The federal government is required to maintain such things as the post office and the census, which necessarily require spending, and Congress may not make military appropriations extending more than two years. But it is empowered to appropriate money for the "general welfare," a term left undefined. In the twentieth century it has come to be construed so broadly as to encompass a museum dedicated to the memory of Lawrence Welk.

Taxes merely had to be uniform throughout the United States and could not be laid on the exports of any state. The power to borrow, meanwhile, was entirely unlimited, one of the very few powers granted by the Constitution that had no checks or balances.

What did limit the fiscal powers of the new government was the universal consensus, among ordinary citizens and the political elite as well, about the proper and prudent way for a government to act when it came to taxing, spending, and borrowing. This consensus was best summed up, as you might expect, by Adam Smith in *The Wealth of Nations.* "What is prudence in the conduct of every private family," he writes, "can scarce be folly in that of a great kingdom." In other words, governments should finance current expenditures out of current income, save for a rainy day (or, more properly, allow the people to do so by lowering taxes when the budget is in surplus), borrow only when inescapably necessary, and pay back borrowed money as quickly as possible.

Alexander Hamilton, appointed by President Washington to be the first Secretary of the Treasury, moved swiftly to put the new government's fiscal house in order. Taxes were laid. Mostly excise taxes on products like whiskey and duties on imports, these were intended both to fund the new government and provide a revenue stream to service and reduce the new national debt. This debt in turn funded the redemption of the old Revolutionary War debt on a sound basis.

At the beginning the national debt amounted to $80 million, something on the order of 40 percent of the gross national product of the day. But as the government found its fiscal feet after 1795, it ran a deficit only twice until the War of 1812. As the country's economy rapidly expanded, the debt declined in both relative and absolute terms. By 1811 the total debt was only a little more than half what it had been in 1795.

The war, of course, sharply reversed matters. Federal government outlays in 1811 were a little more than $8 million. By 1814 they were more than $34 million. Meanwhile revenues suffered as the ever-tightening British blockade cut sharply into import duties, the main source of government income at the time. In 1814 outlays exceeded revenues by 211 percent.

Hamilton had intended that the Bank of the United States, which he established, should finance deficits incurred by the government, but its charter had expired in 1811, the victim of politics. The government now found itself hard pressed to raise loans to finance the war, because the country's financial markets were still in their infancy and unable to handle the large sums required.

The country's affluent were approached directly, and many responded. John Jacob Astor, already America's richest citizen, subscribed to $2 million worth of government paper. (He drove a very hard bargain, buying the bonds only at a steep discount from their face value. The government, of course, had little choice but to go along with the demands of someone who could easily single-handedly fund 2 percent of the entire national debt.)

*Jackson Does Away With the Debt Once and for Once*

By 1815 the debt stood at $127,335,000, a level it would not see again until the Armageddon of the Civil War. For when peace was again established, the government again determinedly whittled away at that debt. By 1829 it had been reduced to less than $50 million.

When Andrew Jackson entered the White House that year, he decided as a matter of deliberate policy to rid the federal government of debt entirely. By the end of 1834 he was able to announce that he had succeeded. The last of the debt would be discharged, Jackson wrote to Congress in the State of the Union message that year, and the Treasury would have a positive balance of $440,000 on January 1, 1835.

Jackson left no doubt just how important he thought discharging the debt was, equating it with peace itself. "Free from public debt," the President wrote, "at peace with all the world . . . the present may be hailed as the epoch in our history the most favorable for the settlement of those principles in our domestic policy which shall be best calculated to give stability to our Republic and secure the blessings of freedom to our citizens." Praise for Jackson's action on the debt was universal. Roger B. Taney, the Chief Justice, wrote the President that the extinction of the debt was, as far as he knew, unique in the history of nations. Indeed, Jackson's achievement remains singular today.

The Democratic party, for its part, decided to take advantage of the fact that January 1835 was also the twentieth anniversary of Jackson's sweeping military victory over the British at the Battle of New Orleans. It held a banquet to celebrate the two triumphs, although Jackson modestly refused to attend, sending the Vice President in his stead. "New Orleans and the National Debt," the Washington *Globe* wrote, "—the first of which paid off our scores to *our enemies,* whilst the latter paid off the last cent to *our friends.*"

But Jackson's hope of a debt-free federal government lived only briefly. Shortly after he left office, the country plunged into depression, one of the most severe of the nineteenth century. Revenues, which had reached $50,827,000 in 1836, shrank to $24,954,000 the following year. Until the depression lifted in 1843, the government would have only one year of surplus as the debt climbed back up to $32 million. The Mexican War then caused a further rise, to $68 million.

It was in 1847, during the Mexican War, that Congress for the first time altered the practice of appropriating specific amounts of money for each expenditure it authorized. Instead it empowered the Treasury to pay all interest and principal on the national debt as it came due, regardless of the amount paid out. This raised little comment at the time. After all, there was no choice about paying the money if the ability to borrow at reasonable rates was to be maintained, and it saved Congress the trouble of passing a specific bill every year.

For many years this was the only federal spending that was put on what a later age might call automatic pilot. In the twentieth century, however, Congress would resort more and more to this so-called backdoor spending, until it became one of the prime reasons the budget went out of control.

After the Mexican War the peace and prosperity of the early 1850s allowed the debt to be cut in half. Then a new depression struck in 1857, and the debt moved back up until, at the end of 1860, it amounted to $64,844,000. Only one year later it reached $524,178,000 and was rising at a rate of well over a million dollars a day.

### Modern Funding for Modern Wars

The Civil War was by far the largest war fought in the Western world between the end of the Napoleonic era and World War I, and its cost was wholly without precedent. To pay for it, the federal government moved to tax nearly everything. Annual revenues, which had never exceeded $74 million before the war, were $558 million by 1866 and would never again drop below $250 million.

But revenues did not come anywhere near to matching outlays, especially in the early years of the war. In fact, 1862 would be the worst year ever—so far—for spending in excess of income: The deficit amounted to an awesome 813 percent of revenues (almost four times the worst year of World War II). Radical new methods were needed to meet the emergency.

It was a Philadelphia banker, Jay Cooke, who invented the means by which modern wars have been financed ever since: the national bond drive. Offering bonds in amounts as small as fifty dollars, Cooke peddled them retail to hundreds of thousands of ordinary citizens, most of whom did not even have bank accounts.

So successful was he that by the end of the war he was actually raising money faster than the War Department could spend it.

By 1866 the national debt stood at a then-staggering $2,755,764,000, no less than forty-two times what it had been only six years earlier. Once again, however, the emergency over, the government began doggedly to pare it down, running a surplus of 7 percent in 1866, and would not have a deficit year— through good times and bad—until the severe depression of the 1890s produced one twenty-eight years later. By then the national debt had been reduced by nearly two-thirds in absolute dollars. As a percentage of the rapidly expanding GNP, it declined at an even faster rate, to well under 10 percent.

The same pattern repeated in World War I and its aftermath. The debt rose by a factor of twenty during the war and was reduced by more than a third in the 1920s. But again government revenues and outlays moved to a new, permanently higher plane, as they have after every great war in our history. With the exception of 1865 the government never spent even close to a billion dollars in one year until 1917. Since that year it has never spent less than $2.9 billion.

Still, the old consensus held. Andrew Mellon, Secretary of the Treasury for most of the 1920s, explained that "since the war two guiding principles have dominated the financial policy of the Government. One is the balancing of the budget, and the other is the payment of the public debt. Both are in line with the fundamental policy of the government since its beginning."

But it was not to hold much longer. In the 139 years encompassing the period from 1792 to 1930, the federal government ran a surplus ninety-three times and a deficit forty-six times. Beginning with 1931, however, we have had a surplus in only eight years and a deficit for the rest (except in 1952, when spending exactly matched revenues).

### FDR Changes the Rules

What happened? One answer, of course, was the Great Depression. World trade collapsed, corporate profits vanished, the incomes of the rich—the only people to feel the personal income tax in those days—steeply declined, and government revenues plunged. More than $4 billion in 1930, they were less than $2 billion in both 1932 and 1933. Meanwhile, government outlays rose sharply as cries for federal relief funds became undeniable:

$3.3 billion in 1930 and $4.7 billion in 1932, when the deficit amounted to 142 percent of revenues, by far the worst peacetime deficit in the nation's history.

Herbert Hoover, true to the old wisdom, tried desperately to do something about the mounting deficits. In 1932, in the teeth of both a re-election campaign and a still-collapsing economy, he pushed a large tax increase through Congress to help balance the books, an act that not only deepened the depression further but ensured his overwhelming defeat in November.

Franklin Roosevelt largely based his presidential campaign that year on lambasting Hoover's fiscal mismanagement. "Let us have the courage to stop borrowing to meet continuing deficits. . . ." Roosevelt said in a radio address in July. "Revenues must cover expenditures by one means or another. Any government, like any family, can, for a year, spend a little more than it earns. But you know and I know that a continuation of that habit means the poorhouse."

No sooner was he in office himself, however, than Roosevelt made an unbalanced budget a matter of deliberate policy for the first time in the history of the Republic. His advisers quickly convinced him that "passive deficits," not profligate spending, were, under the circumstances, good policy. They should be tolerated, the advisers thought, because any attempt to balance the budget would only make matters worse, as Hoover's taxes had, and might even threaten domestic stability.

In any event, despite his campaign rhetoric, Roosevelt—who possessed in spades the gut political instincts that Hoover completely lacked—was not about to continue the policies that had destroyed Hoover's Presidency. He had no trouble discerning that new spending programs were politically popular while new taxes most emphatically were not. Thus the extraordinary conditions of the 1930s allowed Roosevelt to institute an array of new federal programs, doubling federal spending between 1933 and 1940, while raising taxes only on what was left of the very rich, who saw their income tax rates increase sharply.

These spending programs proved enduringly popular even as better times began to return. So the increased tax revenues the improved economy brought were applied largely to extending the new social safety net, not to balancing the budget, still less to reducing the debt. Furthermore, the percentage of the gross national product that passed through Washington began to climb sharply. Federal outlays amounted to 3.7 percent of GNP in 1930.

By 1940 they were 9.1 percent. It is perhaps not going too far to say that Roosevelt changed the country's perception of the proper scope of the federal government's responsibilities as much as the Civil War had changed the country's perception of itself.

It was World War II, however, not New Deal programs, that finally ended the Depression. And needless to say, the war only increased the deficits. By 1946 the United States had run sixteen straight deficits. The national debt now stood at $271 billion, a hundred times what it had been at the end of the Civil War and almost seventeen times what it had been in 1930.

But now, for the first time after a great war, debt reduction was not the first object of federal budgetary policy. The most influential economist since Adam Smith, Britain's John Maynard Keynes (Lord Keynes after 1942), had appeared on the scene. American government fiscal policy would never be the same again.

### In the Long Run We Are All Dead

Before Keynes, economists had been largely concerned with what is now called microeconomics, the myriad individual allocations of resources that determine prices and affect markets. In effect, economics had been concerned with the trees. Keynes, however, looked at the forest, the macroeconomic phenomena of aggregate demand and supply.

Keynes argued, in one of his most famous aphorisms, that while these must balance out in the long run, it was equally true that in the long run we are all dead. In the short run, aggregate supply and demand often do not balance, with pernicious results. If demand outstrips supply, inflation occurs. If total demand is insufficient, depression results.

Keynes further argued that government could and should take an active role in affecting both aggregate demand and supply. When inflation threatens, Keynes thought, government can dampen demand by reducing the money supply, raising taxes, reducing government spending, or some combination of the three. Opposite government action could deal with an economic slowdown. The result, thought Keynes, would be a smoothly functioning economic system, permanently high employment, and low inflation.

Equally important, Keynes stood Adam Smith on his head with regard to debt. He argued that families and nations are different economic beasts altogether and that prudence for one could indeed be folly for the other. A family, Keynes said, must necessarily borrow from someone else, but a nation can borrow from itself, the debits and credits canceling each other out, at least macroeconomically. The national debt—that often necessary but always undesired evil of classical economics—therefore didn't really matter.

There is no doubt that Keynes's theory is a mighty work of a mighty intellect. Keynes published his seminal book, *The General Theory of Employment, Interest, and Money*, in late 1935, and it had an immense impact throughout the intellectual world. It is not hard to see why. Like Adam Smith and unlike all too many other economists, Keynes commanded the English language. Moreover, his theory appeared to solve many puzzles regarding how the Great Depression had come about and why it lingered so long. But as a prescription for handling the economy in the future, it has proved to have at least three fatal flaws.

The first is that Keynes still viewed the economic universe as economists had always viewed it, as a machine. Economics became a discipline in the eighteenth century, when Sir Isaac Newton's intellectual influence was overwhelming. As a result, economists from Adam Smith on have looked to the Newtonian clockwork universe, humming along in response to immutable laws, as their model for the economic universe.

At the end of the nineteenth century, an Englishman named Alfred Marshall, trained as a mathematician and physicist, created what Keynes—Marshall's pupil at Cambridge—approvingly called "a whole Copernican system, by which all the elements of the economic universe are kept in their places by mutual counterpoise and interaction." Marshall's conception was self-regulating and inherently stable. Keynes substituted one that required an engineer—government—for maximum efficiency. Keynes's model has dominated economic thinking ever since, despite the fact that even enormously expanded and refined, it has proved inadequate at best and often quite useless in predicting events in the real world.

The reason is simple enough. The unspoken assumption of the economy-as-machine paradigm is that a given action with regard to taxes, spending, or monetary policy will have a given result, just as putting more pressure on the gas pedal always makes a car move faster. Unfortunately the basic parts of an economy are not bits of metal obeying the laws of physics but human beings, often unpredictable and always self-interested.

So the cogs in the American economy—you, me, and 250 million other human beings—are capable of interacting in ways unexpected by economists using mechanical models. That's why a 1990 tax on luxury boats and airplanes, which was supposed to raise $16 million, raised $58,000 instead. People simply stopped buying boats and airplanes. Rather than raise revenue, the new tax caused ten thousand layoffs. To use the car analogy again, this time stepping on the gas pedal didn't make the car speed up; it made the oil pressure drop.

The second flaw in the Keynesian system is that timely and reliable information on the state of the economy is essential if politicians are to make correct policy decisions. But even in a world filled with number-crunching computers this is not to be had. Final figures of even so basic a statistic as GNP come out three years after the period they measure. Preliminary figures, to be sure, are available in a few weeks, but they are highly unreliable and subject to gross revision. It's a bit like driving a car whose dashboard instruments tell you only what the situation was an hour earlier.

The third flaw in Keynes's theory lies in human nature itself, a powerful force in the real world that Keynes totally ignored. For the Keynesian system to function, it must be applied dispassionately. Taxes must be cut and spending increased in bad times. In good times, however, taxes must be increased and spending cut. That, in a democracy, has proved to be politically impossible.

One problem, of course, is that depression is always recognized in real time, but prosperity, like happiness, is most easily seen in retrospect. The 1980s, for instance, are increasingly becoming remembered as a time of plenty in this country, a decade when the GNP rose by 35 percent in real terms. But the newspapers of the day were filled with stories about farmers losing their land, the big three auto companies being taken to the cleaners by the Japanese, and the first stock market crash in nearly sixty years.

In an economy as vast as that of the United States, recession is always going to be stalking one region of the country or one sector of the economy, even while the overall trend is upward. Living day to day, ordinary citizens, politicians, and economic reporters alike have a natural tendency to concentrate on the trees that have problems, not the forest that is thriving.

The flaws, of course, were not apparent in the beginning, only the theory's promise of making a world without depression possible. Economists took to it immediately. Within a decade it was the overwhelmingly dominant school of economic thought.

But there was a second reason that Keynes so quickly swept the field among economists. It might be called the Madison Effect, in honor of James Madison's famous dictum that "men love power." After all, until Keynes, politicians had not *needed* economists. But Keynes made them indispensable, and economists knew it.

## "We Are All Keynesians Now"

Politicians took a little longer to come around. Those of Truman's and Eisenhower's generation, born in the last decades of the nineteenth century, had been raised in the classical tradition, and many had actually read Smith, [David] Ricardo, and John Stuart Mill in their youth. By the 1930s these men were middle-aged and relatively unreceptive to new ideas, especially fundamental ones.

Also, the predictions regarding the postwar American economy by the Keynesians proved very wide of the mark, foreseeing unemployment when inflation turned out to be the major problem. And even Keynesians, using any number of different variations on the Keynesian economic model, gave contradictory advice. Harry Truman joked that what he needed was a one-armed economist, because the ones he had were always saying "on the one hand . . . but on the other hand."

The politicians, however, were also fully aware of the sharply different political fates of Hoover and Roosevelt. Passive deficits therefore were no longer questioned in times of recession, nor are they likely to be again.

And fully Keynesian notions began to creep in. In 1946 Congress passed the first Full Employment Act, committing government to actively seeking high employment in the national economy, something that would have been unthinkable twenty years earlier. That same year the President's Council of Economic Advisers was created, within the White House itself, to offer the President options for handling the economy as a whole.

Still, between 1946 and 1960 there were seven years of deficit and seven of surplus, all but two of the deficits small ones. The fact that two of those years of surplus were during the Korean War demonstrates clearly that the idea of pay-as-you-go still had powerful political appeal. And the national debt, while it did not shrink in nominal dollars (in fact it rose from $271 billion to $290 billion), did shrink by nearly a third when measured in constant dollars. And the economy in these years grew swiftly. So the national debt, which had been nearly 130 percent of GNP in 1946, was less than 58 percent of GNP by 1960.

But if Keynesianism was largely an alien or at least uncongenial concept to those who served under Truman and Eisenhower, it had a powerful appeal for the new generation of politicians who came to power with John F. Kennedy in 1961. They had been educated during the Great Depression and its aftermath. Many had been taught to think economically in Keynesian terms (the first edition of Paul Samuelson's thoroughly Keynesian introductory college textbook, which has sold in the millions, came out in 1948).

And again the Madison Effect exerted a powerful tug. Until Keynes the business cycle had been regarded as a force of nature, no more to be influenced than the tides and thus not within a politician's venue. Now, however, there was an elegant theory that not only justified political manipulation of the economy as a whole but virtually commanded it. By enlarging the scope of legitimate political action, Keynesianism enlarged the power of politicians. By the end of the 1960s, even so basically conservative a politician as Richard Nixon was able to say, without fear of contradiction, "We are all Keynesians now."

Moreover, politicians have a natural inclination to spend in general, even if they might disagree fiercely about what, specifically, to spend on. After all, it earns them the gratitude, and likely the votes, of the beneficiaries. Equally, they hate to tax and perhaps lose the votes of those who have to write bigger checks to the government. Under the old consensus, pleasing both halves of the body politic had been largely impossible, and politicians spent much of their time choosing between them and hoping they guessed right.

Keynesianism gave them an intellectual justification for pursuing their self-interest in both high spending and low taxes. It is little wonder that they did so. Constantly enlarging government spending to meet one more perceived need, they avoided higher taxes either by paying with the increased tax revenues of an expanding economy or by actually increasing the debt, despite the prosperous times.

Since John F. Kennedy was inaugurated as President, the U.S. government has run a budget surplus exactly once. During the first decade of total Keynesianism, the national debt increased by nearly a third (although it stayed nearly flat in constant dollars, thanks to the increasing inflation that marked the latter years of the decade). That was a greater increase than in any previous decade that did not involve a great war or depression. But because the sixties were also a decade of strong economic growth, the debt as a percentage of GNP continued to decline, although at a much slower pace than in the late forties and fifties. By 1970 the national debt was only 39.16 percent of GNP, lower than it had been since 1932.

Keynesians, of course, took credit for the strong economic growth in that decade and pointed to the falling ratio of debt to GNP as proof that debt didn't matter to a sovereign power. Indeed, they talked about being able to "fine-tune" the American economy, mechanics tweaking it here and changing the air filter there to keep it running at peak efficiency.

In fact the Keynesian economic model, or more precisely all the Keynesian economic models, for they were many, were about to run off the road altogether in the high-inflation, high-unemployment economy of the 1970s. It was an economy that Keynesians thought to be impossible in the first place. Meanwhile, political events and new political conditions were beginning to interact in Washington, and the budget of the U.S. government, the largest fiscal entity on earth, was about to spin out of control.

### *"The Most Inefficient and Expensive Barnacle"*

The Founding Fathers deliberately established an eternal power struggle between the President and Congress. They gave to Congress those decisions, such as how much spending to allow, that reflect the diverse interests of the people. Equally they gave the President the powers that are best exercised by a single individual, such as command of the military.

Over the years since Washington took office, power has flowed back and forth between the White House and Capitol Hill several times. In great crises, when a strong hand at the tiller was obviously needed, Presidents like Abraham Lincoln and Franklin Roosevelt were able to get pretty much what they wanted from Congress. So too could Presidents of extraordinary personality or political skills, such as Theodore Roosevelt and Lyndon Johnson. But when times were good or the White House was occupied by a weak President, like Ulysses S. Grant, Congress has tended to steadily encroach on the President's freedom of action.

Nowhere have the power shifts between President and Congress been more noticeable in the twentieth century than in regard to spending. It was only in the aftermath of World War I that the federal government began for the first time to develop an actual budget to facilitate looking at the whole picture, not just the sum of all congressional appropriations. Until 1921 each executive department simply forwarded its spending requests to the Secretary of the Treasury, who passed them on in turn to the appropriate committee in the House. (The Constitution mandates that all revenue bills must originate in the House. By convention, spending bills originate there as well, giving the House the dominant congressional say in fiscal affairs.)

After the Civil War both houses of Congress had established appropriations committees to handle spending bills. Members who were not on these committees, however, envied the power of those who could dispense money—then as now the mother's milk of politics—to favored groups. By the mid-1880s eight of the fourteen appropriations bills had been shifted to other committees. A former chairman of the House Appropriations Committee, Samuel Randall, predicted disaster. "If you undertake to divide all these appropriations and have many committees where there should be but one," he wrote in 1884, "you will enter upon a path of extravagance you cannot foresee . . . until we find the Treasury of the country bankrupt."

Time would prove Randall right, in fact more than once. By 1918 some departments had appropriations that were decided on by two or more committees, often working at cross-purposes. Many in Congress were disgusted with how such important matters were handled. "The President is asking our business men to economize and become more efficient," Rep. Alvan T. Fuller declared in 1918, "while we continue to be the most inefficient and expensive barnacle that ever attached itself to the ship of state."

In 1920 the House, by a bare majority, restored exclusive authority on spending bills to its Appropriations Committee, and the Senate followed suit two years later. But the House Appropriations Committee was considerably enlarged and split into numerous subcommittees that dealt with the separate spending bills. The committee as a whole usually had no practical choice but to go along with the subcommittees' decisions. Power over individual appropriations therefore remained widely dispersed, while the ability to control and even determine total spending remained weak.

Meanwhile, in 1921 Congress passed the Budget and Accounting Act. This established the Bureau of the Budget, an arm of the Treasury Department, and the General Accounting Office, an arm of Congress empowered to audit the various executive departments and to make recommendations for doing things cheaper and better.

The executive departments now had to submit their spending requests to the Bureau of the Budget, which put together revenue estimates and a comprehensive federal spending plan before the requests were transmitted to Congress. By establishing the Bureau of the Budget, Congress gave the President dominating influence over overall spending. Because Congress lacked the bureaucratic machinery, it had no choice but to accept the President's revenue estimates and could do little more than tinker with his spending proposals.

In 1939 Roosevelt, to tighten his grip on the budget even further, moved the bureau into the White House itself, where it would be under his immediate thumb. (In 1970 it became the Office of Management and Budget [OMB].) In 1946 Congress, wanting to increase its own power over the overall budget, passed the Legislative Reorganization Act. This required Congress to decide on a maximum amount to be appropriated each year before the actual appropriations bills were taken up. It was a dismal failure. In 1947 the Senate and House failed to agree on a spending limit. In 1948 Congress simply disregarded the limit and appropriated $6 billion more than the spending resolution had called for. In 1949 it failed to produce a resolution at all.

And Congress has often acted in ways that actually reduced its power to affect the budget as a whole, by increasing the amount of so-called backdoor spending. The members of the legislative committees still resented the power of the Appropriations Committee and its subcommittees, and in the late 1940s they began to redress the balance by writing spending into permanent law. Thus any changes in spending levels in the programs affected would have to pass through the committees that originated the laws in the first place.

They did this by authorizing government agencies more and more to borrow on their own, to enter contracts, and to guarantee loans that then become obligations of the United States. Some quasi-governmental agencies such as the Postal Service were taken "off budget" and thus effectively removed from direct political control. But the most worrisome of this backdoor spending has been the "entitlements"—moneys paid without limit to all who qualify, in such programs as Social Security, food stamps, and Medicare. Today backdoor spending constitutes fully three-quarters of the entire budget but receives no direct congressional control whatever.

Congress's failure to set total spending limits in the 1940s left the President still largely in charge of the budget for the next two decades, thanks to his ability to forecast revenues and shape the overall budget and, increasingly toward the end of the period, his power of "impoundment." The Constitution is completely silent on whether the President is required to spend all the money that Congress appropriates. Certainly George Washington didn't think so; he was the first to impound a congressional appropriation by simply refusing to spend it. Most Presidents, up to Richard Nixon, did likewise.

In 1950 Congress even indirectly acknowledged a limited impoundment power, by authorizing the President to take advantage of savings that were made possible by developments that occurred after an appropriation was made. But as the pressure on Congress to spend increased, and the old pay-as-you-go consensus began to fail, Presidents were forced to use the impoundment power more often and more aggressively in order to keep total spending in check.

In 1966 Lyndon Johnson used impoundment to cut a huge $5.3 billion chunk out of a $134 billion budget. His aim was to damp down the inflation that was largely caused by his guns-and-butter policy of fighting the Vietnam War at the same time he was increasing social spending at home. The impounded money included $1.1 billion in highway funds and $760 million in such popular areas as agriculture, housing, and education. The Democratic-controlled Congress, needless to say, was not happy about this. But since Johnson was both a Democratic President and perhaps the greatest political arm twister in the country's history, he was able to enforce his way. In the following two years he impounded even larger sums.

His successor, Richard Nixon, did not fare so well. Nixon was, as he said, a Keynesian. But as a Keynesian he knew that in times of high inflation and low unemployment, such as he faced when he entered office, it was time to tighten, not increase, federal spending. Mostly by coincidence, in 1969, Nixon's first year, the budget that was largely the work of the outgoing Johnson administration produced the last surplus the country has known.

Thereafter, congressional appropriations, despite the good

times, continued to rise, and Nixon impounded more and more money. During the election of 1972 he called for a $250 billion spending ceiling for the next fiscal year, but the Senate rejected the request in October. Winning forty-nine states the following month, the reelected President decided to keep federal spending under that limit anyway, using the explicit power of the veto and the implicit one of impoundment.

Congress reacted angrily. Rep. Joe Evins, who was chairman of the Appropriations Subcommittee on Public Works—the very ladle of the political pork barrel—claimed that Nixon had impounded no less than $12 billion in appropriated funds. The Nixon administration responded that it was impounding only $8.7 billion, the smallest amount since 1966.

The Senate convened hearings on impoundment, chaired by Sen. Sam Ervin of North Carolina, the Senate's leading authority on the Constitution, who thought that impoundment was flatly unconstitutional, being in effect a line-item veto. Both the House and the Senate produced bills that would have severely restricted or even eliminated the President's impoundment authority. But no impoundment bill cleared Congress that session, and Washington was soon consumed with the Watergate scandal. As Nixon's political leverage began to erode, Congress set out to make itself supersede the Presidency in the budgetary process. The result was the wildly misnamed Budget Control Act of 1974. Nixon signed it on July 12, not because he thought it was a good idea but because he knew any veto was futile. Less than a month later he resigned, leaving the Presidency weaker than it had been in the forty years since Franklin Roosevelt had been inaugurated.

*The Madison Effect*

The new Budget Control Act created the Congressional Budget Office to give Congress much the same expertise as the President enjoyed from the Office of Management and Budget and, of course, duplicating most of its work. Further, it forbade impoundment, substituting two new mechanisms, recision and deferral. The first allowed the President to request that Congress remove spending items from appropriations. But unless both houses agreed, the money had to be spent. Needless to say, recision has proved useless as a means of budgetary discipline. The second mechanism, deferral, was ruled unconstitutional.

But with the Presidency already severely weakened by the

folly of its most recent occupant, Congress, in writing the Budget
Control Act, was much more concerned about the distribution of
power within Congress itself. The original proposal of the joint
committee that had been established to review budget procedures
called for ceilings to be established early in the year. These, of
course, would have restricted the ability of Congress to begin new
programs or enlarge old ones without taking the money from
somewhere else, so flexible "targets" were substituted for rigid
ceilings.

The result was that there was now little to offset Congress's
natural inclination to spend, either in Congress or in the Presidency. Further, this inclination had been, if anything, only increased by a revolution in the House of Representatives that resulted in the overthrow of the seniority system.

Under the seniority system the senior member of a committee
in the majority party was automatically chair of that committee.
This setup had been arranged in the early days of the century as a
check on the then unbridled power of the Speaker. But the many
freshman representatives who entered the House in 1975, in the
wake of the Watergate scandal, were typically young, liberal, and
not eager to wait years before achieving real power in the House.

They forced a change in the rules so that the majority-party
caucus (all members of that party meeting together) elected the
committee chairs at the beginning of each new Congress. In practice this meant the Democratic caucus until this year, since the
Democratic party had had a majority in the House from 1954.

In theory this made the House much more democratic. In fact
it removed nearly the last check on spending. Under the seniority
system the committee chairs, safe both in their seats and in their
chairmanships, could look at the larger picture—the national interest—as well as their own political interests. Under the new
system, however, they had to secure the support of a majority of
the caucus every two years to keep their chairmanships. That, of
course, meant they had to make promises—and promises, in
Congress, almost invariably mean spending. Further, the spread
of television as the dominant medium for political campaigns,
and the political-action-committee system for funding those campaigns, made the members of Congress increasingly independent
of their home base and grass-roots support and ever more dependent on the spending constituencies that ran the PACs.

The result was an explosion of deficit spending, because there
was no one in Washington with the power or the inclination to

stop it. In nominal terms, the national debt more than doubled in the 1970s, from $382 billion to $908 billion. In constant dollars, despite the galloping inflation of that decade, it rose more than 12 percent. And while as a percentage of GNP it had been falling every year since the end of World War II, in the 1970s it stayed nearly constant by that measure.

The only thing that kept federal deficits from getting a great deal worse than they did was the very high inflation the nation experienced in the late 1970s. The inflation caused nominal wages to rise sharply, while real wages declined. Regardless, the ever-higher nominal wages pushed people into higher and higher tax brackets. It would seem that it would have been a politician's dream come true: a mammoth and continuing tax increase on real wages that didn't have to be voted on.

But, of course, Lincoln was right, and it is not possible to fool all of the people all of the time. When Ronald Reagan ran for President in 1980 on an antitax, antigovernment platform, he swept out of office an elected President for the first time in forty-eight years and the Democratic majority in the Senate, for the first time in twenty-six. But while Reagan was able to push through both tax reduction and reforms—indexing brackets, for instance, so that inflation no longer automatically raised taxes—he achieved real spending limitations only in the first year of his Presidency. Thereafter his budgets were declared "dead on arrival" as soon as they reached Capitol Hill.

And Congress provided no coherent substitute. Indeed, more than once Congress was unable to enact a single appropriation bill before the start of the fiscal year, October 1. To avoid shutting down the government, it had to pass so-called continuing resolutions that allowed federal departments to continue spending at current levels.

President Reagan was determined to fund the Star Wars project he initiated and to continue the buildup of the military that had begun in the Carter years. He was able to get these expensive programs through Congress, and they finally helped bring victory in the Cold War. But Congress was unwilling to cut spending elsewhere, while the cost of the now-myriad entitlement programs ratcheted upward in real terms year by year.

So federal spending continued to rise without relation to revenues. The result, coupled with the huge bailout required by the savings and loan debacle, was an avalanche of deficits. In the 1980s debt again more than tripled in nominal dollars, as it had in the 1970s. But this time inflation did not cushion the blow nearly so much, and debt more than doubled in real terms. As a percentage of GNP the national debt increased from 34 percent to 58 percent, the highest it had been in three decades.

Numerous "summits" and "budget deals" between the President and Congress were held in the 1980s and 1990s, and numerous "reforms" were agreed upon. But none of them addressed the root of the problem. Indeed, 1985 was the year the budget deficit became a major political issue and the first of the laws meant to bring spending under control, known as Gramm-Rudman, was enacted. But that year Congress also initiated no fewer than 54 *new* government benefit programs, bringing the total number to 1,013.

Stripped of rhetoric, the attempts to rein in spending amounted to little more than business as usual today with spending cuts promised for tomorrow. None of them produced any lasting reversal of the trend of higher and higher deficits. In the first three years of the 1990s the debt-to-GNP ratio rose another 10 percentage points, to more than 68 percent.

The reason was simple enough. The self-interest of members of Congress in getting re-elected had become intimately intertwined with more and more spending—the quid pro quo of PAC contributions—at the price of prudence and the national interest. The utter congressional domination of the budget process therefore ensured that spending would only increase.

In 1992, with the people clearly unhappy with how the country's affairs were being handled, Bill Clinton ran for President on a platform of "fundamental change." A minority of a deeply divided electorate chose him and his platform, rejecting an elected President for only the second time since Hoover lost to Roosevelt sixty years earlier and giving a third-party candidate a higher percentage of the vote than any third-party candidate since Theodore Roosevelt ran as a Progressive in 1912.

But an ossified congressional majority, while paying lip service to restraint, in fact resisted any change in the status quo of how Congress worked, because it would have meant a change in their power. The Madison Effect held them in its grip. The very day after the 1992 election, the congressional leadership flew to Little Rock and advised President-elect Clinton to downplay the congressional and structural reforms that were part of his program, in order to get the rest enacted.

Clinton in what turned out to be one of the biggest political misjudgments of the twentieth century, agreed. It was to be business as usual in Washington for two more years. But only two years, it turned out. Still another "budget deal" with Congress to curb the federal government's spending addiction was worked out in 1993, but it was a near carbon copy of the 1990 budget deal that had been an unmitigated failure. This time the Republicans would have none of it, and it passed with no GOP [Grand Old Party or Republican Party] votes whatever. Indeed, the recent decline in the size of the federal deficit, widely touted as the result of the newest budget deal, has been in fact largely due to the sale of assets taken over from failed S&Ls. Even the Clinton administration predicted that the deficit would begin rising again soon.

The people reacted unequivocally at the next opportunity, and the 1994 congressional election was a political earthquake of the first order, one whose aftershocks will rumble through Washington far into the future. The Democratic party lost its majority in the House for the first time in forty years. The Speaker of the House lost his seat, the first time that had happened since the Civil War, and many other "old bulls" went with him. The Senate as well went Republican, along with many state governorships and legislatures.

As soon as the new Congress convened on January 3, 1995, it began to change the system, beginning with extensive reforms of procedures in the House.

It is far too soon to know how profound the revolution begun last January will prove to be. After all, those who have to change the status quo—the members of Congress—are the prime beneficiaries, at least in the short term, of that status quo. The Madison Effect ensures their reluctance to transfer some power over the budget to the President or to end the inherently corrupt system of funding presidential campaigns. But we do know that human nature cannot change; it can only be taken into account as our understanding of it deepens. The Founding Fathers, the greatest practitioners of applied political science the world has known, realized intuitively that the self-interest of politicians must be made, by law, to lie in the same direction as the national interest if the government is to work in the interests of the people for long. If, in searching for the answers to the political problems of the late twentieth century, we have some measure of the same political wisdom, all will be well.

## HOW TO SHRINK THE U.S. BUDGET
## DEFICIT[2]

There is a very serious problem faced by our one-year-old grandson, Jacob, and our country. I am referring to the fact that over the past three decades our nation has been spending beyond its income by the staggering amount of four and one-half trillion dollars.

This fiscal year ending September 30, 1995, the deficit will be about $192.5 billion. Any one of us could solve the deficit problem in less time than my talk today. The problem is getting the 100 Senators and 435 Representatives in the U.S. Congress to agree to do it.

This year, the government will take in $1,346.4 trillion in taxes and receipts and it will spend $1,538.9 trillion. That pesky little $192.5 billion difference represents this year's federal deficit. To put this in perspective, the total economy of the U.S. in 1994 was about $6.7 trillion. Federal spending consumes 23 percent of our annual gross domestic product and taxes 20 percent. That means our annual deficit is 3 percent of our gross domestic product.

If you add this year's deficit to all the previous deficits, our public debt will total $4.9 trillion at the end of this fiscal year. That is 73 percent of our annual domestic product. The debt bomb is growing at the rate of $10,000 per second. Those who would minimize the burden of the debt point out that several other countries have debts larger than ours in relation to their GNP: Japan, Canada, Italy and the UK.

In 1981, we had a $3 trillion economy and a $1 trillion national debt. By 1986, we had a $4 trillion economy and a $2 trillion debt. By 1992, we had a $6 trillion economy and a $4 trillion debt. By 1996, we will have a $7 trillion economy and a $5.3 trillion debt. It is finally dawning on everybody that the national debt is growing much faster than the economy.

The federal government has been spending beyond its means

[2]Speech delivered to the Kenna Club of Santa Clara University, CA by George Marotta, research fellow, Stanford's Hoover Institution, on September 15, 1995 from *Vital Speeches of the Day* 62/1:13–6 O 15 '95. Copyright © 1995 by George Marotta. Reprinted with permission.

for so many years now. The budget has been in deficit for 37 of the last 41 years (1954–1995). Surpluses have been scarce—only 4 years and the largest surplus was only $4 billion back in 1956. Economist John Maynard Keynes argues for the use of fiscal policy to stimulate or retard the economy, but he had in mind an equal use of deficits and surpluses. What we have been doing is irresponsible. With the value of our dollar in recent sharp decline, it just might be that Will Rogers' prediction will come true: "We'll show the world we are prosperous, even if we have to go broke to do it."

As a nation, we are getting deeper in debt every year. The fastest growing programs in the federal government are the entitlement programs for the elderly which represents 70 percent of all spending increases. The Medicare program will become insolvent in five to seven years.

Another rapidly growing item in the federal budget is interest on the national debt, which this year will total $234 billion (15 percent of the federal budget). Last fiscal year the interest on the debt of $203 billion was exactly equal to the 1994 deficit: $203 billion.

If you want to get angry, think about this statistic: our government will collect from us in individual income taxes $588 billion this year. Forty percent of that (or $234 billion is required just to pay interest on previous deficits). When you next look at your pay stub, multiply your withheld taxes by forty percent and that's what goes for interest alone.

If government programs actually solved problems, citizens would be more tolerant of paying taxes. After 30 years of fighting poverty, the number of people living in poverty has increased an average of ten percent annually from 1967 to 1993, even while spending increased. We spend annually on poverty programs, two and a half times the dollars needed to raise all recipients above the poverty level!

The government is so big and complex that there are many conflicting programs. The federal government gives financial assistance to areas impacted by defense installations. Now that we are cutting military bases, we now have a federal program that provides assistance to areas losing bases. We provide help to farmers which increases food costs which increases government funding for poverty programs.

The national debt amounts to $18,846 for each person in our country assuming a population of 260 million including children and retired persons. The burden is greater if you apportion the debt only on people who are working. The current $40,000 of debt for each family will go up to $10,000 over the next four years.

Just think, Jacob, our new grandson born in October 1994, is already deeply in debt to the tune of $18,846! Annual interest at 7 percent will cost $1,316 a year on his portion of the national debt. Of course, next year there will be interest on the interest. When I was born in 1926, my country gave me a birth-gift of only $140 of the national debt and my annual interest was only $9.80. When my first son was born in 1953, we gave him a birth-gift of $1,663 of national debt and $116 of annual interest charges.

The debt was created from all the previous federal government budget deficits that were incurred throughout history. For example, the expense of World War II was financed partly through deficits. Our recent presidents make World War II deficits look like 30-day charge accounts. Our biggest deficit then was $55 billion. Recent deficits have been staggering. The largest was in 1992 when we went $290 billion into the red. Since then the deficit has been dropping, but the forecast is that the debt will rise from $200 billion in seven years to $400 billion in ten years.

There is a lot of talk in Washington, D.C. about cuts in federal spending. However, fiscal year 1965 (three decades ago) was the last time federal spending was less than the previous year. The only decrease prior to that was in 1955 and 1956 during the Republican controlled 83rd Congress—when Eisenhower was president. In the sixty-six-year period since 1929, the federal government has spent more each year than the prior year except for 7 years (five of those years were following World War II and the Korean War). In the same sixty-six-year period, taxes have increased every year except 9. The last year that federal tax receipts have gone down was in 1983 as a result of the Reagan tax cut.

Federal spending is out of control because the forces advocating increased spending far exceeds the forces favoring reduced spending and a balanced budget. The principal culprit is us—"we the people" who want all the "goodies" government provides but we don't want increased taxes. Second to blame are our elected officials who win their positions by promising to assist (i.e., to spend our money for) carefully selected interest groups. Congress instinctively wants to "do good." H. L. Mencken said it this way, "The politicians know what the public wants and plan to give it to us good and hard."

The third problem is the bureaucrats. A few years ago, the

number of people working for government at all levels exceeded all the workers in the manufacturing sector of our economy. All of the incentives of bureaucrats is toward self-preservation and more spending and the growth of bureaucracy. They earn much more than the average taxpayer and soon lose touch with the "grass roots." They are strongly entrenched and in total numbers have become quite a force in politics. Have you heard the one about the civil servant found sobbing at his desk in the Department of Agriculture? He explained to an inquiring friend that he just learned that "his farmer had died."

The fourth problem is the media. They emphasize (and often exaggerate) problems which adds more pressure for remedial actions by government. Local problems are immediately brought to national attention rather than being solved locally. Disaster relief assistance is the latest "pandora box" to add to our federal deficit problem.

The fifth pressure group for more government are lobbyists in our nation's capital who lead the charge in the "gimme" attack on the deep-pocketed Uncle Sam: labor, teachers, businesses, etc., etc. The lobbyists are invariably seeking more "government" because some among us are demanding it. Washington, D.C. is a most attractive watering hole as the principal dispensing station for financial assistance from the federal treasury.

The federal government is so large and complex and powerful that when it makes a mistake, it can do great damage. In the Waco fiasco, Secretary of the Treasury Benson said he did not know about the raid as it was Attorney General Reno's responsibility.

Enough of past statistics and the problem of the deficit, the question is how are we going to balance the budget? The answer is simple: we must raise taxes and/or cut spending.

O.K., let's look first at taxes. No matter what the government tries to eke out of the working people, statistics show that since 1965 they could only get from us an amount that equals about 19 percent of the gross national product. That seems to be our level of tolerance for paying for government. No matter what they think inside the beltway, we work to support ourselves and our families, and not to pay taxes!

Tax-the-rich schemes won't fix the deficit problem. The top one percent are now soaked pretty heavily: they pay 25 percent of all individual taxes. And the world outside the Beltway knows that higher tax rates merely force capital to seek tax shelters.

The deficit problem is caused by a spending increase which is faster than the rate of inflation and since 1965 has amounted to about 22 or 23 percent of our GNP. The last real cut in spending was twenty years ago in fiscal 1965 (right before the Vietnam War.) After 1965, spending really got out of control and we have had big deficits ever since. In the mid-60s we had a national debate on whether we should have guns (Vietnam War) or butter (the Great Society program). Our leader (LBJ) [Lyndon B. Johnson] decided that we would have both, plus put a man on the moon by the end of the 60s, AND pay for much of it LATER.

We know that government is not going to raise taxes because the voters sent a big message to Congress last November that they want taxes and government reduced. The House of Representatives (who all get elected at the same time) got the message and passed a Balance the Budget Amendment. The Senators (many of whom were not up for election last year) did not get the message and they defeated the amendment.

It would have imposed a Constitutional ban on deficit spending after 2002, except in emergencies and when approved by a three-fifths super majority vote. Even if it had passed, Congress would still have to decide what to cut.

The inflation of the 1970 decades contributed to our current problem. That inflation pushed us all up into higher tax brackets and gave Congress billions of additional tax dollars without any legislation. They proceeded to do what legislators enjoy doing— they spent it! According to economist Keynes they are supposed to run budget surpluses during good times.

One study prepared by the advocates of the Constitutional amendment shows that if you limit spending INCREASES to four percent per year (the rate of inflation 3 percent plus population growth 1 percent) over the next seven years to 2002, the budget will be in balance at the end of that period. That assumes that federal receipts will continue to grow at a little over 6 percent per year, that has been its growth rate from 1986–1994.

Another device which would help keep spending under control is to give the President a line-item veto so he can cut lesser priority projects (also known as "pork") from being sneaked through as part of other more important legislation.

It is a widely accepted fact today that the cost of living index is overstating the inflation rate by about one-half percent. That is costing our society billions in increased government benefits and wage increases. Indexing wages and benefits has been a monumental failure in our society because those increases merely fuel another round of increases in the future. Inflation would be under more control if it were not indexed and all of us had a stake in preventing inflation.

I personally do not think Congress has the guts to bring the budget into balance. You will recall that they had schemes in the past to try to control deficit spending.

First, they set limits on how high the national debt could go, and they still do that. The problem is that every time that number is reached, they pass legislation to permit it to go higher. Congress must do that to permit the Department of the Treasury to issue more government bonds to finance the debt.

Second, in 1985, Congress passed a scheme sponsored by Graham-Rudman-Hollings to reduce the budget deficit to zero over a six-year period. You may recall what happened to that fine plan. Half way through the process Congress increased spending and talked the "read my lips" President (George Bush) into raising taxes, which later cost him his job.

I personally think that the Constitutional Amendment (an external control device) is necessary to force Congress to restrain spending. We the voters tell our own representatives to "go in there and get all the goodies you can for us."

Congress people need to have some excuse to tell us why they could not get as much as we wanted because of the need to balance the overall budget.

When Senator Warren Rudman, the New Hampshire Republican announced in April 1992 that he was not running for reelection, he blamed it on Congress' inability to deal with the budget deficit. "This is not the fiddler fiddling while Rome burns. This is the entire orchestra playing while Rome burns," he said. He placed a lot of blame on everyone including citizens who think there is such a thing as a free lunch.

The recent resignations of moderates such as Senator Bill Bradley of New Jersey and Representative Norman Mineta of California confirms the belief that government is not the answer to solving all of our societal problems.

More and more citizens are learning how government really works: The Senate gets the bill from the House. The President gets the bill from the Senate. And the fed-up taxpayers get the bill from everyone!

I believe that government is best which governs as close to the people as possible. The federal government has deep pockets because of its ability to print money and run huge deficits. Because of that and the tendency of politicians to buy votes with promises of expanded or new programs, we have developed a type of "gimme" government which has made millions of our citizens dependent upon the delivery of checks by postal vehicles all over our nation on the first day of each month. Have you noticed that the wealth inside those trucks are causing more postal stickups?

As a student of public administration, I know that the closer that programs are located to the people the more effective they are and the more value we receive for a dollar spent. One wag described sending dollars to Washington, D.C. as similar to a man giving himself a blood transfusion from his left arm to his right arm. The problem is that the hose has a big leak in the middle— meaning the costly government bureaucracy!

This Congress has decreed that the federal government will not "mandate" that state and local governments carry out programs unless federal funds are provided. State and local governments will pick up some of the programs which are being discontinued on the national level. If the people in certain areas choose not to continue a federally-discontinued program, that is their right.

The decentralization of government provides many benefits. Programs which work in one area might be emulated in another. States which overtax their citizens with unpopular programs will get immediate feedback and adjust accordingly. Unlike the federal government, state governments must balance their budgets as they cannot print money or run deficits. States have another control which the federal government does not have. Financial institutions give quality ratings to bonds issued by states. That requires states to be fiscally responsible.

Another major reform is that we need to revise our archaic federal tax code. A flat-rate tax proposal has been developed by Alvin Rabushka and Robert Hall, senior fellows at Stanford's Hoover Institution. Under their 19 percent flat tax, all income would be taxed once and only once. It would be very fair to all Americans but particularly to low-income earners because it would permit a tax-free allowance of $25,500 for a family of four. The family would pay a tax of 19 percent on its earnings above that allowance. Millions would no longer pay any income tax. All wage earners would pay less tax than under the current system.

Most importantly, the flat tax would save taxpayers hundreds of billions in direct and indirect compliance costs. It would shift billions from investments that reduce taxes to those that produce goods and services. The tax would help to balance the budget because it would give an enormous boost to the economy by dramatically improving incentives to work, save, invest, and take entrepreneurial risks.

Today's heavily-burdened taxpayer will not be very much amused to learn that during the legislative debate in 1913 leading up to the 16th Amendment (giving the federal government the right to levy taxes directly), one legislator recommended that an upper limit be placed on the tax rate. He was laughed down by the sponsors who stated that the revenues needed would never exceed a tax rate of one or two percent! The marginal personal income tax rate, which is now close to 40 percent, once hit a high of 90 percent. Which led one devout citizen to remark, "If ten percent is enough for the Lord, it ought to be good enough for the IRS!"

If government is shrunk on the federal level, the state and local levels may take up some of the slack. There is a growing perception that many government programs have not worked and should be discontinued. Many were based on the false assumption that every problem has a governmental solution—an idea promoted by bureaucracies and special interest groups.

We are currently planning to move the welfare program from the federal to the state level together with block grants to help with the funding. This problem has been too complex for the federal government to solve. Decentralization will allow the states more latitude for experimentation.

Many legitimate societal needs will not be met by government at all, which brings in the private sector. If the government takes less in taxes, families will be more capable of taking care of themselves and of contributing to the welfare of others.

Much needs to be done to balance the U.S. budget, but if all else fails, here is my prescription to force Congress to do the correct thing: (1) Freeze their salaries until the budget is in balance; (2) Better yet, reduce their salaries by the percent of the deficit. This year they would suffer a 13 percent pay cut (the $192.5 billion deficit divided by a $1.5 trillion budget); (3) Cut off the air conditioning in their chambers during the hot Washington, D.C. summers; (4) Set the thermometer at 50 degrees during the winter months; (5) Discontinue the withholding method of paying taxes from salary and wage checks and go back to the old-fashioned way—in a yearly lump sum; (6) Require that members of Congress be required to prepare their own tax returns by hand (make them eat their own cooking); and lastly (7) Set the salary level of members of Congress to be inversely related to the size of their staffs.

The tax-paying, working class is fed up with government as usual. Corporate restructuring is forcing most Americans to work harder to retain their jobs or to find new ones. While struggling to keep their heads above water, they see bureaucrats spoonfeed the recipients of government entitlement and pork programs. The middle class is suffering from compassion fatigue and is demanding that the agenda be radically changed.

In summary, the solution to the deficit problem is simple: reduce government spending by $200 billion, from 23 percent of GDP to 20 percent, which equals the current level of taxes that citizens currently tolerate. It won't be a disaster as it simply means slowing the rate of increase of spending (not really cutting at all).

We are finally reaching a national concensus on the need to eliminate the deficit. House majority leader Gingrich wants to do away with the deficit in seven years. In 1992, Clinton said he would balance the budget in five years. Recently, he said it will take ten years. After Gingrich said seven, Clinton said maybe we could do it in nine.

After three decades of deficit addiction and spending with federal plastic, withdrawal is going to be very painful. There must be an equal distribution of pain; no sacred cows should be exempt, not even Social Security should be "off the table."

The "full faith and credit" of the United States of Amèrica is not as full or as faithful as it once was. Continued deficit financing is reckless, and if continued will create serious inflation and endanger our pensions and savings. Indeed, the whole financial future of everyone's savings for retirement and other major goals is at stake.

We need to adopt a constitutional amendment to require a balanced budget, give the president a line-item veto to carve out the pork, enact a fair and simple flat-rate income tax, and decentralize government programs to be closer to the people. Most importantly, we the people need to take responsibility for our own lives and to provide more direct person-to-person help to members of our family and other people in our communities who are in need. Also, we should elect representatives who understand and have the guts to act on an age-old message, recently reaffirmed by the overthrow of communism: "The less government we have, the better . . ." (Ralph Waldo Emerson).

It's amazing that we have allowed the central government to grow to such monstrous proportions in light of our historic rebellion against repressive government. Have we so soon forgotten Thomas Jefferson's dictum, "The natural progress of things is for liberty to yield and government to gain ground." or Thomas Paine's, "Government, even in its best state, is but a necessary evil." We will be a better society when we make government the last resort to solving our problems, and not the first.

In the coming debate on balancing the federal budget, let's hope that the voices of wealth-creating entrepreneurs drown out those who want only to redistribute other people's money. A society that is more concerned about the redistribution of wealth than about its creation will produce only an equality of poverty as recent history has shown.

If, and it's a BIG if, this Congress and President really pulls it off and begins acting fiscally responsible (for a change), I can just see Jacob wildly swinging his noisy rattle. Why, even this grandfather would give a little "toot" on his noise maker.

---

## WHY THE DEFICIT? A HANGOVER FROM '80S BINGE[3]

---

Some people claim that the continued existence of the deficit proves that the government's appetite is always out of control: Something in Washington—maybe the water—forces congresses and presidents to always push spending beyond reasonable limits. But when I look at where the deficit comes from, I see that such claims are not true.

Our current federal deficit is the hangover from the borrow-and-spend bender that the government tied on in the 1980s. If we had balanced the budget since 1981, we would now have no deficit.

[3]Article by Lloyd Bentsen, former Secretary of the Treasury, from *The Wall Street Journal* A18+ N 3 '94. Copyright © 1994 by Dow Jones & Company, Inc. Reprinted with permission.

For example, let's look at our projections for the current fiscal year [1995]. We now project that during fiscal 1995 the federal government will collect $1.354 trillion, or 19% of national income, in taxes. It will spend $1.297 trillion on all programs combined, or 18% of national income. The federal government will take in $57 billion more than it spends on all programs combined, from Social Security and Medicare to the FBI, from unemployment to the Air Force.

Why then a deficit? Why do we not project a $57 billion surplus? Because substantive programs are not the only checks written on the Treasury. In addition, I have to pay interest on the outstanding national debt.

As of the end of President Carter's last budget, fiscal 1981, the total national debt amounted to $785 billion. This debt is still outstanding—every time we have had to pay off one of the bond issues that were outstanding at the end of fiscal 1981 we have raised the money by borrowing again. In fiscal 1995, we are going to spend $51 billion in interest on that portion of the national debt that pre-dates the budgets of the 1980s.

But if the pre-1981 debt were our only national debt, as would be the case if we had balanced our budgets throughout the 1980s, we would still be running a surplus: The $57 billion excess of revenues over spending would provide enough to pay the interest on the pre-1981 debt, with $6 billion to spare.

But in addition to the debt that existed at the end of fiscal 1981, $785 billion, there is an extra $2.648 trillion of debt that has been borrowed since. The interest we owe on this post-1981 portion of the debt is $174 billion in the current fiscal year [1995], or more than our entire projected deficit of $167 billion.

It is because the interest bill from the 1980s exceeds . . . [1994]'s deficit that I say that our current deficits are not the result of an inherent and omnipresent out-of-control government appetite. Instead, they result from the borrow-and-spend policies that ran up $2.665 trillion in national debt since the end of fiscal 1981.

In the 1980s we went on a national bender, cutting taxes and raising defense spending, without making provision for the long-term fiscal soundness of government. Now we have a national hangover, a $2.665 trillion debt hangover that gives us $174 billion of interest payments and this year's $167 billion deficit headache.

It was a heck of a bender, it is a heck of a hangover, and— for a Treasury secretary at least—it is a heck of a deficit headache.

We are no longer on our bender—revenues are more than enough to cover program spending. But we still have the hangover and the headache. How should we deal with the headache that is the remaining deficit?

Some politicians seem to want to propose the hair-of-the-dog approach, another round of unfunded tax cuts and defense-spending increases, on the premise that if it felt good in the early 1980s maybe it will feel good enough in the late 1990s to make us forget our hangover. But I can't recommend that. If we tried it, I would feel very sorry for whoever is Treasury secretary a decade from now. That individual will have five times the debt-and-deficit headache that I do.

I recommend that we take some aspirin and go about our business. Indeed, that's what President Clinton asked us to do in his 1993 deficit-reduction plan.

We do feel much better: . . . . OMB [Office of Management and Budget] Director Alice Rivlin and I released our two agencies' final report on the deficit in fiscal 1994—the period from Oct. 1, 1993, to Sept. 30, [1994] . . . . The federal deficit was down to $203 billion.

When Mr. Clinton took office, we projected that—if the administration did nothing—the deficit would be $302 billion in fiscal 1994. It is extremely good news that the president's leadership in cutting spending, the positive response of the economy to the president's plan, and some good luck on technical matters that affect spending together gave us a fiscal 1994 budget deficit that is nearly $100 billion lower than we feared. And it is extremely good news that, because of the president's deficit-reduction program, we are now projecting that the current fiscal year [1995] will see a deficit of $167 billion or so, or 2.4% of America's total national income, half the size of the 4.9% of GDP [Gross Domestic Product] deficit of 1992.

The past five years have seen two substantial deficit-reduction programs enacted, in 1990 under President Bush—who demonstrated real courage then in putting the long-run health of the American economy above his own political career—and under President Clinton's leadership in 1993.

As we go about our business, let's never forget that the source of our headache today is not anything we are doing today, in terms of federal revenues and program spending, but the result of our having really tied one on in the last decade.

---

## OFF BALANCE[4]

---

Like a villain in a bad horror movie, the balanced budget amendment pops back to life every time it is killed. The proposal was defeated by only twelve votes in the House on Thursday [March 17, 1994]—just weeks after it was rejected by the Senate—encouraging its supporters to gear up for another try next year. The amendment is bad economics, but it will keep coming back until we debunk the economic myths perpetuated by the debate.

Foremost, we need to understand what the national debt is and is not. It is not something we owe to other countries; it is a debt of the government to its own people. Abraham Lincoln had it right in his 1864 annual message to Congress: "Held as it is for the most part by our own people, it has become a substantial branch of national, though private, property . . . . Men can readily perceive that they cannot be much oppressed by a debt which they owe to themselves."

Government debt is, in effect, the exact opposite of private debt: The greater a person's debt, given his assets, the less his net worth; the greater the government's debt, the greater the people's net worth.

The national debt is not the $4.4 trillion figure so often cited, but is really what the government calls the "gross federal debt held by the public," some $3.3 trillion. (This properly excludes over a trillion dollars of accounting entries that the Treasury Department makes for accumulated surpluses in Social Security and other government trust funds.)

Less than 20 percent of the debt is owed to foreigners, and that percentage has been coming down; it was over 21 percent before the big deficit years of the 1980's. Since the debt is over-

---

[4]Article by Robert Eisner, professor of economics, from *The New York Times* A23 Mr 19 '94. Copyright © 1994 by The New York Times Company. Reprinted with permission.

whelmingly owed to Americans—as individuals or through pension funds, businesses, banks, insurance companies and state and local governments—it does not represent borrowing from the future or a burden on our children. The debt or liabilities of the government are the assets of the American people, assets that will be bequeathed to our children.

The balanced budget amendment's chief sponsor, Senator Paul Simon of Illinois, makes little sense when he argues that instead of having "invested in its future, we are the first generation . . . to borrow from its future." We might just as well say that the government has given the American people $2.4 trillion of interest-earning assets to bolster their purchasing power and that of their children.

There is also no sense to the repeated assertion that we are "at the brink of bankruptcy." No sovereign government can be bankrupt as a result of debt in its own currency. The government's debt consists of paper—savings bonds and Treasury bills, notes and bonds, promising to pay in dollars. The government can always get dollars, printing them if necessary—and that is far from necessary now nor will it be in the foreseeable future. The only way it could be forced to default on its obligations would be through an amendment prohibiting it from making additional outlays or borrowing.

The real issues lie elsewhere, and they stem from the fact that the government's debt is the liquid assets of the American people. The greater these private assets are, the wealthier Americans will perceive themselves to be, and the more likely they will be to spend. Greater spending means increases in sales, profits, orders for production and hiring of workers.

It is true that if an economy is booming and employment is relatively full, with no more resources available to increase production, higher spending will result in inflation. If this happens, the Federal Reserve would raise interest rates to fight inflation, thereby reducing investment. But now, with unemployment still close to seven percent and indications that our brisk recent growth may be slowing, is no time to reduce spending. More spending, not less, will increase investment and consumption as business expands to meet growing demand.

Senator Simon is correct in saying that we are not taking care of ourselves and our future. Crime ravages our cities. Tens of millions of Americans are without health insurance. The environment is deteriorating. Much of a generation is growing up functionally illiterate. We *are* putting a grave burden on the next generation. But a balanced budget amendment will do nothing to eliminate these real deficits.

---

## HOW TO BALANCE THE BUDGET— FOR REAL[5]

---

No question about it. We must get the federal budget deficit under control. Talk about government waste. Some 14% of all federal spending is thrown away each year paying the $203 billion in interest on our $4 trillion national debt. And that ever-expanding waste of money will ultimately cripple the economy if we continue spending around $200 billion more than we bring in annually. This nonsense has to stop.

But how? Up to now, the raging national debate about how best to balance the budget sounds like a talk radio shouting match: Soak the rich! No! Dismantle the welfare state!

What's needed is a dispassionate look at what it will take to get ourselves out of this mess. Before we can address the deficit, we have to understand where our money goes each year. In addition to the $203 billion for interest, the government shells out $21 billion for international aid (1.5% of all federal spending), $231 billion for domestic programs, including education, transportation and law enforcement (17%) and $294 billion for defense (19%). The major share of the budget, though, is absorbed by entitlements; they total $762 billion (49%), including $302 billion for Social Security, the biggest government program of all.

Those numbers illustrate a couple of inescapable conclusions:

1. The deficit nearly equals all domestic spending combined. Therefore, if we tried to balance the budget by slashing domestic expenses alone, we would have to eliminate virtually every program—shut down the FBI, stop maintaining our highways, close our national parks.

2. That points us to the big money in the major entitlement programs. But again, if we cut every penny of entitlements to the

    [5]Article by Frank Lalli, managing editor of *Money* magazine from the January 1995 issue of MONEY. Copyright © 1995, Time Inc. Reprinted with permission.

poor—and slashed benefits for the wealthiest too—we would still be in the hole for $170 billion a year by the end of the decade.

For the most part, entitlements don't go just to the poor or to the rich. At last count in 1990, virtually half of all American families got an average of $10,300 a year in entitlements, which include veterans' benefits, unemployment insurance and government pensions as well as Social Security and Medicare. And the more you earn, the more you're likely to get: families making less than $10,000 collect just $7,880 in benefits, vs. $16,190 for those making more than $150,000.

So, what can we do to cobble together the huge spending cuts we need? We can begin by recognizing that we will all have to do our share. The sooner we acknowledge that, the sooner the national debate will shift to choosing the wisest reductions and, yes, the fairest tax increase to get the job done.

After reviewing the budget plan recently proposed by Sens. Bob Kerrey (D-Neb.) and Jack Danforth (R-Mo.) of the Bipartisan Commission on Entitlement and Tax Reform, as well as other proposals, we've compiled the following list of options. Our list concentrates on actions that would not only deflate the deficit but would also spread the sacrifices as widely—and equitably—as possible. For the sake of comparison, we've noted each option's deficit-cutting contribution in 1999, when the annual shortfall is projected to be $251 billion.

- **Tax all entitlements.** After every taxpayer receiving entitlements. Average tax increase: $1,500 a year. 1990 savings: $68.1 billion.
- **Eliminate the mortgage interest deduction.** Affects 27 million homeowners. Average hike: $1,900. Savings: $62.1 billion.
- **Progressively reduce entitlements for middle- and high-income households.** Affects recipients with incomes above $40,000. Average cost: $3,800 a year. Savings: $47.9 billion.
- **Eliminate the deduction of state and local income taxes.** Affects anyone who pays local income taxes and itemizes. Average tax hike: $980. Savings: $47.3 billion.
- **Adjust the government's CPI calculation to reduce annual inflation adjustments to benefits and income tax brackets.** Affects every taxpayer and every recipient of inflation-indexed entitlements. Average cost: $135 a year. Savings $5.6 billion. (The savings increase significantly as the cumulative effect of lower inflation adjustments builds in later years.)

## BALANCED BUDGETS AND
## UNREASONABLE EXPECTATIONS[6]

**Question.** Republican control of the House and Senate has produced a radical transformation in many areas of federal policy. It's been outlined in the "Contract With America" and the fiscal year 1996 budget resolution. In terms of federal budget issues, have Congress and the White House moved more deeply into the realm of economic fantasy, or have they come closer to objective reality?

**Answer.** I think we are all operating deep within a land of fantasy. The expectations of Americans are unrealistic. We want balanced budgets and lower taxes. At the same time, we wish to preserve important, rapidly growing entitlement programs like Medicare and Social Security. Moreover, many of us want the nation to do all of this while simultaneously maintaining a strong defense. Some even advocate an increase in defense spending. These desires are clearly contradictory. We can't achieve all these objectives at the same time.

**Q.** Since the budget debate is on center stage now, let's focus first on it. Have we made any progress on the deficit? Are you optimistic or pessimistic about the prospects?

**A.** The public and many members of Congress are convinced that the answer to the first question—what have we accomplished to date?—is that Congress and the White House have done very little to address the deficit problem. Nothing could be further from the truth. In the spring of 1990, we faced a tremendous and rapidly worsening structural imbalance. The federal government's spending commitments, particularly those imbedded in the large entitlement programs, were growing far faster than the revenues that would be generated from current tax laws. In response to this problem, Congress passed large, multi-year deficit-reduction packages in 1990 and 1993. Together, those packages

⁶Interviewee Robert Reischauer, former Director of Congressional Budget Office, from *Challenge* 38/5:4–11 S '95. Copyright © 1995 by M. E. Sharpe, Inc. Reprinted with permission.

have resolved roughly half of the underlying problem that existed in the spring of 1990.

**Q.** Are you speaking of just the structural part of the deficits?

**A.** Yes. We have resolved roughly one-half of the long-run structural imbalance that existed in 1990. With the economy operating at or a bit above full capacity, which is the current situation, the cyclical component of the deficit has disappeared. The remaining structural imbalance is still extremely large and growing and will be very difficult to resolve. But no knowledgeable observer would say that we haven't taken several giant steps in the right direction. Unfortunately, all the relatively easy ways to reduce the deficit have been used by the 1990 and 1993 budget packages. They included tax increases primarily on the upper-income groups and significant reductions in defense spending. With the November elections, these two ways to reduce the deficit are no longer politically viable. We are going to have to search elsewhere to solve the second half of the deficit problem.

**Q.** What do you mean by the "structural deficit?" And what were the rough orders of magnitude involved?

**A.** The actual deficit has a structural and a cyclical component. The structural deficit is that which would occur if the economy were operating at its full capacity and the tax revenues and spending reflected the strong position of the economy. When the economy is operating below its potential, revenues are depressed, and spending on certain programs such as unemployment compensation and food stamps are elevated. This is the cyclical component of the deficit. The Congressional Budget Office [CBO] projects that the deficit for the current fiscal year—1995—will be about $175 billion. Since the economy is operating slightly above full capacity, it means that the structural deficit is at least $175 billion and probably closer to $190 billion.

**Q.** Was the structural deficit larger in 1990?

**A.** As a percent of potential GDP [Gross Domestic Product], yes, but not by much. The deficit-reduction measures adopted in 1990 and 1993 kept the structural deficit from ballooning. We will not see the full effects of these measures until 1998. Without these measures, we might have had structural deficits twice as large as we now project in the last half of the 1990s.

**Q.** So the structural deficit was pushing the federal government deficit toward the $500 billion mark by the end of this century, but Congress and the White House intervened and managed to reduce it. Which measures were used?

**A.** We significantly restrained the growth of discretionary spending, raised taxes, and cut Medicare and other entitlements a bit. No reduction in federal spending or increase in taxes is ever popular or easy, but these were the most politically acceptable actions available because the ways we did them left the middle class largely unscathed. As a result of the caps placed on discretionary spending—that is, the spending that is determined annually by the thirteen appropriation bills that Congress must pass—this component of the budget has fallen from 9.2 percent of GDP in 1990 to an estimated 7.7 percent of GDP in 1995. This drop is attributable exclusively to the reduction that has taken place in the defense budget, which declined from 5.5 percent to 3.8 percent of GDP. Discretionary spending for domestic programs actually increased from 3.3 percent to 3.6 percent of the GDP over this period. The only reason we have been able to reduce our defense budget as quickly and as significantly as we have is that the Soviet Union fell apart; in other words, Mikhail Gorbachev played a major, if unrewarded, role in the American deficit-reduction effort. The military establishment that we had built to protect ourselves from the "evil empire" was no longer needed. That historical development was a clear, justifiable, and relatively easy rationale for reducing federal spending.

**Q.** What about the tax side of the equation?

**A.** That was the second major thrust of the deficit-reduction packages of 1990 and 1993. We raised taxes, but we didn't raise rates across the board or inflict much pain on the middle class. We raised taxes largely on the top income groups in the country. As a result, total effective tax rates for the richest 20, 10, and 5 percent of the population are back close to the levels that existed before Ronald Reagan took office. In other words, on this dimension, the tax component of the Reagan revolution, which was embodied in the Economic Recovery Tax Act of 1981 (ERTA), was a short-lived revolution from the perspective of upper-income groups. Because the tax hikes of 1990 and 1993 affected a relatively small number of Americans in a significant way, they were politically acceptable. But politicians will have a difficult time going to this well again. The justification for the tax increases of 1990 and 1993 was that the wealthy had benefitted disproportionately from the tax breaks of the Reagan era. Therefore, the rich could be asked to contribute significantly to resolving the deficit problem. Now that effective tax rates for upper-income groups are close to their pre-Reagan levels and Congress is controlled by Republican majorities, there is no chance that increased taxes on the rich will be a significant part of any package of deficit-reduction measures. The Congress, in fact, is bent on reducing taxes in ways that would benefit upper-middle-income and upper-income families the most.

The third element that Congress relied on heavily to reduce the deficit in the 1990s was reductions in provider reimbursements in the Medicare program. This was politically acceptable, of course, because the beneficiaries of the Medicare program (who far outnumber the providers) were largely unaffected. Beneficiaries did not suffer any reduced access to providers of health care or any other consequences of reduced payments going to hospitals and doctors. While medical providers were certainly upset about the reductions in their federal reimbursements, they had ways to compensate for their losses. They could increase the volume of services they performed for other payers, increase their charges to other insurers, or try to wring efficiencies out of their production processes. But a revolution has swept through the health sector of the economy during the last few years. Private insurers are bargaining aggressively and negotiating lower prices from providers. Faced with new competitive pressures, providers are trying to be lean, mean, and more efficient; they have less fat now. From the perspective of the budget cutters, this means that providers will be more resistant than in the past to reductions in federal Medicare payments, and beneficiaries may feel the impacts of such cuts. So here we are in mid-1995. We still have half of the problem that existed in the spring of 1990 to resolve if we want to balance the budget. And we have used all of the relatively easy solutions. This leaves Congress and the President facing some very difficult choices.

**Q.** Even though the Republican Congress is talking about deficit reduction, isn't their focus on tax cuts and military spending hikes much like a repeat of the early 1980s? Didn't ERTA open up the structural deficit to begin with in 1981?

**A.** The budget resolution calls for an increase in defense spending above the levels requested by the President, but this does not mean that the Pentagon will be in fat city. Under the budget resolution's limits, the Pentagon will have a budget in 2002 that has 17 percent less purchasing power than the budget it has for 1995. The tax cuts are still only a promise. Under the rules contained in the budget resolution, spending cuts sufficient to balance the budget in 2002 under the baseline economic assumptions will have to be approved by the various committees before the Senate Finance Committee will be allowed to report a tax cut bill. The committees may come up short, in which case there will be a smaller tax cut or none at all. In the end, Congress may decide to trade the tax cut for smaller reductions in popular programs like Medicare. If there is a tax bill, the danger is that the revenue losses are backloaded, that is, they are small in the first few years and then grow rapidly in the years beyond the five- or seven-year focus of the budget resolution.

**Q.** Is a balanced budget possible with a tax cut?

**A.** It can be done, but it will be very difficult. Spending cuts will have to be deeper than would be the case if there was no tax cut. It will take considerable cooperation between a Republican-led Congress and the Democratic President to do it. Right now, there are few signs of such cooperation.

**Q.** But President Clinton also has tax cuts in mind. Doesn't that suggest at least the prospect of cooperation on tax issues?

**A.** There are some important differences in terms of size and emphasis between the tax cuts in the "Contract With America" and the President's proposals. The President has suggested much smaller tax cuts and ones directed at providing relief to the middle class. The Republican tax cuts are larger, provide more relief to upper-income groups, and emphasize reduced taxes on capital income.

**Q.** Aren't the Clinton tax cuts for the family supposed to be revenue neutral? Aren't they covered by spending cuts or other revenue increases?

**A.** The tax cuts have to be viewed in the context of the overall budget proposals. Both the budget-resolution plan and the Administration's revised budget would reduce the deficit. Therefore, the tax cuts are "paid for" by spending cuts. These spending cuts are made up of deep reductions in discretionary spending and substantial cuts in the entitlement programs. We could either reduce the deficit by more or cut spending less if we decide to forego the tax cuts. Public opinion polls show that the American public is more concerned about cutting the deficit than it is in getting a tax break. The public is also very concerned about the depth of the cuts proposed for Medicare and some other programs. In fact, the public places a higher priority on protecting Medicare from cuts than on reducing the deficit.

**Q.** Let's clarify the point made at the outset. If Congress and the White House did nothing now, we would come to the end of the decade and still not have a balanced budget. What would the bottom line look like, if we passed all of the changes called for by the budget resolution?

**A.** If we do nothing more, we will have a substantial deficit by the turn of the century—about $300 billion or 3.3 percent of GDP. The policies called for in the budget resolution would lead to a budget that was close to balanced by 2002. I say "close to" balanced because of all of the uncertainties. It could be a deficit or surplus of $50 billion at that time. The estimates behind the budget resolution are pretty honest. Unlike some past budgets, this plan does not contain much blue smoke and mirrors. As of mid-July [1995], one has to be guardedly optimistic that the Congress and the President will agree to legislation that reduces future deficits substantially. That is a quite different outlook than anyone would have bet on before the November 1994 elections. In October of 1994, the common assumption was that nothing more would be done to cut the deficit until after the 1996 presidential election. The change in the party in control of Congress changed the outlook entirely. To their credit, the Republican leadership and the two Budget Committee chairmen have worked hard to formulate, pass, and fulfill a budget plan that could get us close to a balanced budget by the year 2002.

**Q.** So you don't believe that the Republicans are about to repeat the experiment of the early 1980s that opened up the structural deficit?

**A.** I'm hopeful that history won't repeat itself, but there is always that danger. The Republicans, many Democrats, and the President are schizophrenic. They want a balanced budget and lower tax burdens. These goals are in conflict. Deeper spending cuts are the only way to resolve the conflict. But this resolution requires inflicting considerable pain that the American people don't want to bear. If politicians are unwilling to do this, and instead substitute procedural promises such as spending caps for concrete legislative changes, or if they decide to push the pain off until the final years of the plan, we could well end up watching the sequel to the 1981 fiscal horror classic, "Escape of the Deficit Monster." Alternatively, the tax cut could be abandoned or reduced to some small size. Then again, we could see nothing happen this year except the deficit reduction contained in the constrained appropriation bills for 1996. The effort to cut mandatory programs could bog down in Congress, or the President and Congress could get into a stalemate that results in no enacted reconciliation bill. But as of mid-July, hopes are still high; it is the stated intention of both the Republican leadership and the President to enact measures that will reduce the budget deficit substantially and cut taxes.

**Q.** And how will this compare to what was done in 1990 and 1993?

**A.** The proposal is to cut the deficit entirely through spending reductions. This is in stark contrast with the 1990 and 1993 deficit-reduction packages. Tax increases played an important role in past deficit-reduction packages. Tax increases made up 35 percent of the policy-related (as opposed to debt-service reductions) deficit reduction in 1990 and 62 percent of the deficit reduction in 1993. So the task will be much harder in 1995; we're going to reduce the deficit by more than we did in either 1990 or 1993, and we're not going to rely on any revenue enhancements. As I said before, defense will be cut from current levels. But the contribution of defense will be nowhere near as large as it was in the past. Much more of the heavy lifting in the current plan is to be done by the entitlement programs and the nondefense discretionary programs.

**Q.** Where will all those spending cuts in other programs fall?

**A.** Well, there is general agreement that Social Security will not be cut. If the budget resolution's guidance is adhered to, real non-defense discretionary spending will be reduced from current levels by 31 percent by 2002 and real defense spending will be down 17 percent. Medicare will have to be cut about 21 percent from its projected baseline level in 2002; Medicaid will be cut by a bit over 30 percent; and the other mandatory programs such as student loans, farm price supports, welfare, and government pensions, by over 12 percent. If all of these cuts are made, we will have a very, very different federal government than any that the American people have lived with since at least the mid-1950s.

**Q.** A "very, very different" government? In which respects?

**A.** One possibility is that the government would be operating an array of programs much like the ones it operates now, but at significantly reduced levels. Another is that certain activities which the government engages in now will not be undertaken at all. Another possibility is that the federal government discharges its responsibilities in quite different ways. For example, if AFDC, Medicaid, and food stamps are converted into block grants, the system of open-ended matching grants for income maintenance that has existed since the New Deal will come to an end.

**Q.** None of what you've said so far addresses the problem of health-care financing. Isn't it the health-care spending that is really driving the budget deficit?

**A.** It has for some time, and it still is. Moreover, it will continue to do so in the future. CBO's budget projections show that virtually all of the growth in the deficit that is expected in the future is attributable to the two large federal health-care programs—Medicare and Medicaid. Spending in these programs is expected to grow at close to 10 percent per year over the next decade. These programs as the only major budget components that are projected to grow faster than GDP itself—faster than the economy as a whole.

**Q.** Aren't the Republicans planning to cap the spending levels for Medicare and Medicaid?

**A.** The budget resolution calls for sharp reductions in both of these programs. These reductions will be the toughest parts of the resolution to fulfill. Medicare is very popular, and it will be difficult to wring $270 billion out of the program over the next seven years, as the resolution calls for. With respect to Medicaid, the cuts are deep, and states will be left holding the bag because the health needs of the low-income population won't decline when the federal government cuts its contribution. Public hospitals and health clinics depend heavily on Medicare and Medicaid. Will states make up the lost federal payments or close these facilities? The choices won't be easy. Many states are deluding themselves if they think that they will be able to get along fine with less federal money if they have to comply with fewer federal rules and regulations. The depth of the proposed cuts far exceeds the magnitude of any efficiency savings they could realize.

**Q.** Given the demographics of an ever-growing population of people beyond age 65, caused by men and women living longer and by the absolute numbers increasing, won't the demands on the health-care system by those who are retired increase qualitatively as well as quantitatively?

**A.** A considerable gap exists between the 5 percent growth in nominal GDP and the 10 percent anticipated growth in Medicare. If we could just lop off a couple of percentage points from the growth of Medicare, we would save tens of billions of dollars per year very quickly. But there is no way to slow spending by as much as the budget resolution calls for without imposing some real sacrifices and pain on those who depend on Medicare. Both beneficiaries and health-care providers will undoubtedly feel it. The notion that cuts of this magnitude can be squeezed out of the system simply by increasing efficiencies or by instituting some structural reforms is wishful thinking.

**Q.** Another striking result of these cuts is that, as the federal government strives to achieve economies in the financing of health care, more and more of the responsibilities will be falling to the state and local governments. Isn't that the case?

**A.** Yes. In addition, over the last decade or so, the fraction of the population that has had employer-sponsored health insurance has drifted down. That has left more people uninsured. These people are dependent on charity care from nonprofit or public hospitals. Some states have used waivers to expand their coverage under the Medicaid program to pick up some of these individuals. Federal laws have been changed to require and encourage the states to cover more low-income children and pregnant women who lack health insurance. This is one of the factors that has pushed up Medicaid spending in recent years. If Medicaid is transformed from an open-ended matching grant into a block grant, the states will no longer have an incentive to cover more people. States will be paying the full costs for any expansion of Medicaid rather than paying between 20 percent and 50 percent of the cost. In fact, they will have an incentive to cut back their current state contribution. This will probably lead to an increase in the number of uninsured and some degradation of services at inner-city hospitals and other facilities that serve low-income people.

**Q.** Doesn't that mean that, as the eligible population grows in number, both the quantity and quality of care may fall for a lot of Americans?

**A.** More people will go without health services. In addition, those people who get care even though they are uninsured, and those who are reliant on state-funded programs, may receive less-adequate treatment. At the same time, the availability of charity care could decline with the spread of for-profit hospital and managed-care delivery systems.

**Q.** Is there any country in the world that has a model for the kind of system that we seem to be moving toward?

**A.** No.

**Q.** Ours is unique—and uniquely out of control?

**A.** It is uniquely out of control because we have no mechanism for imposing an effective budget constraint on public or private spending, unlike the situation in other countries. But what is most unique and interesting about our system is the way it is now moving into the world of managed care in which for-profit entities are playing an ever more important role. I am not aware of any other situation in the world in which a people has willingly delegated to for-profit entities the job of imposing budget constraints on them for the consumption of a service which is very personal and about which they care a great deal. The model raises some very interesting questions. If the managed-care entity denies the patient the care he or she wants, its profits increase. Because the entity is profit-making, there will always be distrust when the patient is told that a test or procedure that the patient wants is unneeded, inappropriate, or ineffectual. In the long run, the model we are developing may not be politically viable. It would be different if the managed-care providers were nonprofit entities (which some are) or a government agency, neither of which would gain financially from denying care.

**Q.** The great budget retrenchment now underway on Capitol Hill that is being led by House Republicans is founded on a fundamental philosophy that rejects major roles for government that are deeply rooted in American history. They are: (1) macroeconomic management for growth, jobs, and price stability; (2) influencing the degree of fairness, or economic justice, in the distribution of income, wealth, and the economic power that is based on them; and (3) shaping U.S. long-term economic development. What is your perspective on those roles for government?

**A.** Both the economics profession and politicians at all levels of government are becoming more skeptical about the efficacy of discretionary stabilization policy. We have learned that tax cuts and stimulative spending at times of economic weakness often are too little and usually come too late. As a result, they can make the problem worse—not better. Because of the continuous huge budget deficits of the past decade, we have effectively tied our own hands with respect to discretionary stabilization policy. I don't expect that there will be any aggressive federal effort to use fiscal policy to actively manage the macroeconomy any time soon. But at the same time, this doesn't mean that the automatic stabilizers which are built into our fiscal system are ineffectual. Quite the contrary. The structure of the tax system, the unemployment-insurance system, and the food stamp program have all operated in ways to mitigate business cycles. A flat tax, certain forms of consumption taxes, and block grants could undercut the effectiveness of the automatic stabilizers by some small amount.

**Q.** Wouldn't the Republican "Contract" undermine those stabilizers?

**A.** For example, if the Congress were to pass a balanced-budget amendment to the Constitution some time in the future, and the states were to ratify such an amendment, Congress would probably try to change our fiscal system so that spending and revenues didn't fluctuate as much as they do now when the economy rises and falls. That undoubtedly would lead to deeper recessions and to greater suffering during downturns than is the case now. Alternatively, the Congress could decide to run modest surpluses during periods of full employment. When the economy weakened, the surplus would shrink but the requirement for a balanced budget would not be violated.

We can't predict political dynamics in the future. Therefore, we cannot know how rigidly Congress would adhere to a balanced-budget requirement. Obsessions with deficits may fade into history. It is possible that politicians in the future won't be worried about a $20–50 billion deficit that was associated with an economic downturn. But a simple majority would not determine the issue under the balanced-budget amendment that was considered this year by Congress. A supermajority would be needed to break the balanced-budget rule. In a country with wide regional differences in economic conditions, a recession might not affect all areas equally, and so it might be very difficult to muster the two-thirds majority needed to suspend the balanced-budget rule.

**Q.** What about the government's role in pursuing equity?

**A.** Over the past five decades, the federal government has tried a number of approaches to increase economic fairness and improve economic opportunity. The results have not met our expectations, which may have been unrealistic. Some are now arguing that certain programs have, in fact, done more harm than good in that they have created perverse incentives. Economists and policymakers are a lot less optimistic than they were in the 1960s or even the early 1970s. In those years, we thought the government could have a significant and positive impact. Now there is more skepticism, and this has provided the momentum behind the radical welfare-reform proposals that are being considered by Congress and the President's pledge to end welfare as we know it.

With respect to tax policy, we still have a progressive tax system. It is a bit less progressive than it was in the past, in large measure because social-insurance contributions have risen so dramatically. But in considering distributional issues, we shouldn't look at social-insurance taxes by themselves but rather examine the combined distribution of benefits and the dedicated taxes. Looked at this way, the social-insurance programs, by and large, are modestly progressive. The income tax system has become more progressive at the bottom of the distribution, as a result of the expansions that have been adopted in the earned-income tax credit, which provides substantial additional income to lower-income working families. Furthermore, the poorest have been removed from the income tax system entirely by the tax reforms of 1986 and 1990.

**Q.** What about the third role: the federal role in shaping the long-term course of U.S. economic development?

**A.** In this area, we should have a greater degree of humility. There is more agnosticism than existed five, ten, or fifteen years ago. The consensus now suggests that the federal government should try to create a healthy environment in which the private economy can develop, but it shouldn't try to micromanage industries and regions, or to second-guess markets. So, the emphasis now is on creating a stable, low-inflation economy, keeping interest rates low, providing training and retraining for the work force, removing obstacles to occupational mobility, and allowing people of all races and genders to compete on a level playing field. But there is less and less support for policies that have the federal government engaging in regional economic development programs, taking steps to help the machine tool or some other industry, or providing subsidies for export enhancement. The Clinton administration did make some moves in these directions, but the Congress is now busy dismantling these programs.

**Q.** As an observer of the U.S. scene, do you come out as an optimist or a pessimist?

**A.** I'm pessimistic, but not about our political institutions. I think they can work. Our problem is much more a societal one. I think we are a people that doesn't want to invest in order to achieve the good life. We want to be in shape, but we don't want to exercise. We want to express judgments on public-policy matters, but we don't want to read the newspapers. We are a couch-potato society. We want our kids to get into Harvard, but we don't want them to have to do homework in school. Maybe, every older generation sounds this way about the younger people coming along, but we appear to be dominated by an unwillingness to make sacrifices either for the future or to help those who are less fortunate than we are.

Our political system is characterized by 535 independent political entrepreneurs. Some wear Democrat labels; the others wear Republican labels. There's no real party cohesion. These political entrepreneurs owe nothing to their parties. Their parties have no ability to control them. They go out and raise their own money. We look at the new Republicans in the House of Representatives and we must say, "That's different. It's changed. We're in the new world." And, certainly, it appears as if that is the case. But it is too early to celebrate. The question is: Will it last two years or five years? What will happen when the difficult decisions have to be made, when the politicians are called upon to adopt policies that the public doesn't like and place their jobs on the line?

**Q.** Is seven years too short a timeframe to balance the budget? Is ten years significantly different? What are the risks in establishing a timetable of any kind that it will produce slower growth and therefore lower tax revenues than would otherwise be desirable?

**A.** Three factors should be considered when deciding how long to take to balance the budget. The first is the risk that the fiscal restraint associated with the effort poses for continued economic growth. If the adjustment is spread out fairly evenly over the period, a seven-year timeframe shouldn't pose much of a risk. In the budget resolution, the change in the primary deficit as a percent of potential GDP is never as much as 0.6 percent in any year—in most years it is below 0.3 percent. The second factor is the possibility that sharp spending cutbacks could impose an unreasonable amount of hardship on vulnerable populations, shaky state and local governments, and fragile institutions. If the adjustments are phased in gradually, seven years shouldn't cause too much disruption. The final factor is credibility. If the task of balancing the budget is dragged out over too long a time period, it will not be credible. Markets will fear that future Congresses will reverse the spending cuts or tax increases. A seven-year plan has a good deal of credibility—a ten- or fifteen-year plan is less believable.

# II. A CONSTITUTIONAL AMENDMENT

## EDITOR'S INTRODUCTION

Because the money spent in the federal budget affects so many aspects of American life, the methods proposed to abolish its deficits have been equally varied. One proposal that has become increasingly popular involves the passage of a constitutional amendment that would compel the federal government to maintain a balanced budget.

"Economic Impact of a Balanced Budget," the first article in this section, is taken from a Congressional Research Service report. It examines some of the likely effects of a balanced budget, including serious disruption of federal programs as well as private economic activity dependent on them, but concludes that after a phase-in period a balanced federal budget would have long-run benefits for the nation.

The second article, "Trimming the Trillions," focuses on the current deficit and the necessity for finding the political will in Congress to make the necessary spending cuts.

"Balancing the Federal Budget" from *Congressional Digest* supplies an overview of the pros and cons of a balanced budget amendment. Even though such an amendment failed to pass in 1995, it remains a highly debated topic. The next article, reprinted from *The Nation*, claims that a balanced budget amendment would cause such "unimaginably deep cuts in federal spending" that the economy would be crippled.

In "No Courage To Cut," from *Christian Century*, James M. Wall argues that a balanced budget amendment is really an excuse not to cut spending, and that such an amendment would simply permit Congress to pass its responsibility on to the Supreme Court.

The final article, "Attention, Deficit Disorder," written by Jacob Weisberg for the *New Yorker*, contends that while President Clinton cut the deficit nearly in half during the first three years of his term, he has recently dropped his emphasis on further deficit reduction in favor of an election-year middle-class tax cut, the likely result of which will be a rising deficit in 1996 and beyond.

Weisberg says that it makes little sense for the President to "object even to the *notion* of a balanced budget amendment . . . . By endorsing a better version of the plan, the administration would deprive the GOP of one of its best issues for 1996."

## ECONOMIC IMPACT OF A BALANCED BUDGET[1]

Economic arguments for reducing the federal budget deficit rest on dissatisfaction with the nation's economic progress and prospects for the future. They are rooted in a belief that sacrifices to reduce consumption and hence to increase saving are warranted to accelerate future gains in living standards.

The federal budget deficit, together with low private saving, causes a shortfall of total saving relative to investment in the United States. Viewed another way, total demand for borrowed funds by government and private investing exceeds domestic private saving. The resulting high interest rates attract foreign capital to cover the shortfall.

Capital inflows result in spreading foreign ownership of U.S. assets and mounting payments of investment income to foreigners. They also have resulted in trade deficits of unprecedented size. So long as capital inflows continue, trade deficits will persist. If international investors should become unwilling to provide needed capital under prevailing conditions, U.S. interest rates would rise and/or the dollar's exchange value would fall, perhaps steeply, to make U.S. assets cheaper and more remunerative relative to foreign assets. High interest rates resulting from the saving shortfall raise capital costs in the United States and tend to curtail total investment. Lower exchange rates would impose a drag on living standards by raising prices of imports and worsening the nation's terms of trade.

Over the long run, therefore, large federal deficits and low private saving imply increasingly costly and precarious dependence on foreign capital and less investment to modernize and

[1]Article from *Congressional Digest* 74/2:39–41 F '95. Copyright © 1995 by The Congressional Digest Corporation. Reprinted with permission.

expand the economy. They imply smaller gains in productivity and in inflation-adjusted income for Americans. Slow growth since 1973—indeed, no growth or declines in income for many workers and families—already is a source of frustration and anxiety for many Americans and, if continued, may permit other nations to surpass our living standard in the next few years. Federal interest obligations stemming from large, persistent deficits today will make it impossible for future generations to finance expected government services and benefits without elevated taxes and will make their living standards lower than they otherwise would have been.

The goal to enhance productivity means that the budget deficit should be reduced in ways that reduce consumption, not investment, public or private. Closing the deficit by cutting public investment in research and development, education, training, or physical capital, so long as these investments are well conceived, would not serve the economic objectives of deficit reduction.

*Rationale for a Constitutional Amendment*

The rationale for a constitutional amendment to require a balanced budget is that the current budget decisionmaking process shortchanges the welfare of future generations in favor of current generations, and the only way to achieve a more appropriate result is to impose strong constraints on the process. This line of reasoning contains two apparent paradoxes. First, the government already has the power to make all the decisions necessary to balance the federal budget; yet, despite apparent commitment to that objective, it has not used the power effectively to that end. Why not? Second, why would the Congress voluntarily impose limitations on its own decisionmaking power?

Some answers may be found in the economic theory of self-control, which has previously been used to explain some aspects of individual savings behavior. The explanation offered by the theory of self-control is based on the notion that individuals actually have two separate economic decisionmaking personas. One of these "selves" is essentially a myopic consumer, interested primarily in buying as much enjoyment as possible at any given moment. The other "self" is a planner who considers long-term objectives, such as the need to save for a child's future college education or his own retirement.

The individual, aware of both of these inner selves, realizes that the only way to constrain the consumer is for the planner to adopt rules that the consumer cannot easily circumvent. The theory posits that individuals are most likely to impose constraints on their own behavior regarding those decisions for which the benefits and costs occur at different times, especially involving early costs and delayed benefits.

This theory has obvious relevance to the budget decisionmaking problem. There is widespread agreement that the deficit should be reduced. The President and Congress have gone on record many times supporting deficit reduction as a policy goal. But deficit reduction requires current sacrifices in exchange for the promise of future benefits. Despite the apparent commitment ' to deficit reduction, budget decisions have not made consistent progress toward this objective.

Attempting to constrain the decisionmaking options, Congress has adopted increasingly tight limitations on the budget process in the Gramm-Rudman-Hollings legislation and its revisions. So far, however, the rules have not resulted in a balanced budget or a budget that is even nearly balanced. Each time the rules have imposed a serious limitation, they have been changed to lessen the constraint, although the rules in effect since late 1990 have been adhered to and now face increasingly severe tests. The theory suggests that, if self-control does not suffice, rules that are more rigid and difficult to evade are likely to be adopted. Hence, support for a constitutional amendment requiring a balanced budget.

*Reaching a Balanced Budget Under the Amendment*

Ratification of a constitutional amendment requiring a balanced federal budget will not make achieving this goal any less painful than it was before. The hard decisions on what spending to cut, what taxes to raise, whose interest to protect, and whose to sacrifice still must be made, and the impacts will be felt by communities, interest groups, and voters across the country. The constitutional requirement is sought to force the decisions to be made and to make their necessity more plausible to people whose interests are hurt.

The Congressional Budget Office (CBO), in its January 1994 assessment, projected that the federal deficit under present policies would decline from $255 billion in FY [Fiscal Year] 1993 to $166 billion in FY 1996 and then rise again to more than $200 billion in FY 1999 and thereafter. This "baseline" projection assumes that caps on discretionary spending (under annual appropriations) through FY 1998 and limitations on medical entitlements will be observed as envisioned in the Omnibus Budget Reconciliation Act (OBRA) of 1993. That statute also increased taxes.

This is the projected deficit that would have to be eliminated under the proposed constitutional amendment. For purposes of this analysis, we focus on what is required to balance the budget for FY 1998 to FY 2000.

### Uniform Percentage Spending Cuts and Tax Increases

Eliminating the deficit completely by FY 1998 would require closing a gap of some $180 billion; in FY 1999, $204 billion; and in FY 2000, $226 billion. If the entire budget is on the operating table, so to speak, spending cuts and tax increases averaging 5.8 percent would suffice in FY 1998, 6 percent in FY 1999, and 6.4 percent in FY 2000.

Balancing the budget by uniform percentage tax increases and spending cuts across the board would require revenues in FY 1999, for instance, to be $98.4 billion higher. This increase would raise revenues by 1.1 percent of GDP (gross domestic product) above the baseline for FY 1999 and bring total federal revenues to 20.1 percent of GDP, up from 18.3 percent in FY 1993.

To maintain a balanced budget every year, it may be desirable to attain budget surpluses in times of high employment that are large enough to absorb the negative budget impacts of economic recessions without forcing the budget into deficit and requiring Congress either to take actions to offset the budgetary impact of recession or to approve a deficit by the 60 percent supermajorities stipulated in the constitutional amendment. Attaining sizeable surpluses would, of course, require correspondingly larger tax increases and spending cuts during the transition period.

### Implications of Exempting Taxes

Some members of Congress would prefer to cut the deficit while placing major components of the budget off-limits for change. A large group wishes to avoid any increases in taxes, placing the entire burden of deficit-cutting on federal spending. Another large group believes that Social Security benefits should not be curtailed below amounts that will be payable under existing formulae. Precluding or severely limiting changes under major parts of the budget would require correspondingly larger changes in the remaining parts to balance the budget.

Such deep cuts would require basic restructuring of many of the programs affected. This would be especially true for the discretionary programs, for which baseline appropriations already involve substantial reductions in purchasing power. If inflation proceeds at only the 2.6 percent rate assumed in CBO's economic scenario, the purchasing power of discretionary budgets in the baseline would be reduced by an average of 11 percent between FY 1993 and FY 1996 before any new reductions are figured in. The further cuts required in this case would curtail purchasing power of appropriated funds by about 25 percent from FY 1993 levels.

To yield beneficial effects for future economic growth, reductions in the federal budget deficit must increase national saving and investment; in other words, they must reduce consumption without, on balance, curtailing high-priority federal investment or causing reductions in saving or investment by the private sector and by state and local governments. Federal investment is mainly discretionary spending funded under annual appropriations for physical capital, research, development, education, and training, properly channeled through grants to states and local governments. Social Security and other mandatory spending are mainly consumption-generation programs. (Student loan entitlements are in part an exception.) Taxes also can have various effects on private saving.

Most proposals for a balanced budget constitutional amendment stipulate that the budget should be balanced in the second fiscal year after ratification of the amendment by the required three-fourths of the state legislatures. To eliminate a $200 billion deficit within two years, however, could be disruptive to the nation's economy. One cannot know in advance, moreover, whether the economy will be growing robustly, growing slowly, or in recession when the amendment goes into effect. Congress may wish to consider new steps to phase the deficit down during the years in which state legislatures are considering the amendment.

Regardless of how it is implemented, such a budget-balancing program would impose by far the largest and most persistent contraction of the federal budget since the end of World War II and could be expected to seriously disrupt federal programs as well as private economic activity dependent on them, and to exercise a heavy drag on overall production and employment during this period. While the Federal Reserve presumably would offset some of this drag via stimulative monetary policy, it may well not be able to counteract promptly such a rapid shift in the federal budget.

If the economy's growth is slower than assumed, then large spending cuts and tax increases would be required to reach a balanced budget, and the economic disruption would be greater. This possibility calls into question the healthy economic scenario assumed here if a balanced budget is phased in over five or six years and provides arguments in favor of a longer phase-in period. After the phase-in is complete, a balanced federal budget or a surplus, if attained by reducing consumption, could have long-run benefits for the economy's growth by freeing domestic resources for private investment.

---

## TRIMMING THE TRILLIONS[2]

If you equate a balanced budget with a 55-mph speed limit and each $1 billion of deficit spending with an extra mile, the nation is, fiscally speaking, going 258 miles an hour.

That analogy, offered by Rep. Nathan Deal, R-Ga., is just one of the many attempts being made on Capitol Hill to simplify federal finances as a new phase of the balanced-budget debate begins.

Several members participating in the debate over a $1.5 trillion annual budget and a cumulative national debt of nearly $5 trillion try to individualize the debt by noting that each American's share of the red ink has gone from $2,500 to $18,500 over the past twenty years.

Others point out the increasing pace of debt accumulation: It took the country 186 years to reach $500 billion in red ink, but the debt has increased nearly 10-fold in the ensuing thirteen years.

Still others attack the idea of tax increases as an antidote to deficit spending. Taxes rose nearly $700 billion over the past dozen years, but the deficit still went up $3.8 trillion over the same period.

[2]Article by Robert T. Gray from *Nation's Business* 83/6:33–5 Je '95. Copyright © 1995, U.S. Chamber of Commerce. Reprinted with permission.

Those and similar perspectives on the condition of federal finances will be heard with increasing frequency over the next several months as Congress considers proposals for a balanced budget by 2002.

Both the Senate and the House budget committees have developed plans for reaching that goal by relating spending to revenue. That would mean keeping spending $1 trillion below levels now forecast under current laws over the seven years.

Virtually every area of government, with the exception of Social Security, would be affected. GOP [Republican party] leaders have exempted the retirement plan from their budget reductions.

The challenge of bringing spending into line with revenues is particularly stiff in the House, which has approved a five-year, $190 billion package of tax cuts.

The fiscal-policy debate, which will be long and divisive, will contrast the GOP plans with President Clinton's proposed 1996 budget calling for $1.6 trillion in spending and a $200 billion deficit.

The budget committees' recommendations are historically as well as fiscally significant: For the first time since the 1974 budget-reform act creating them, both panels are being led by hardline fiscal conservatives—Sen. Pete V. Domenici, R-N.M., and Rep. John R. Kasich, R-Ohio.

The resolutions produced by these panels set broad spending and revenue goals that require other committees to cooperate by cutting spending in areas under their jurisdictions.

In setting up that arrangement, Congress took yet another in the long series of legislative actions, dating to 1921, through which it has tried to impose long-term discipline on federal spending.

Although Domenici and Kasich are both heading toward budget balance, there are some differences in their respective approaches, including the House tax plan, and there will have to be some give-and-take before final action by the full Congress.

Republicans in Congress had hoped to begin their budget work while a proposed constitutional amendment mandating such balance from 2002 onward was being considered by the states. That proposal, however, fell one vote short of approval in the Senate this spring.

The current budget procedures were designed to impose discipline on budgeting by forcing Congress to weigh proposed total spending against total potential income—a fundamental concept previously absent from federal fiscal planning. The procedures do not require that spending and revenue match, however.

When the budget-reform act was adopted 21 years ago, spending was $269 billion, income was $263 billion, and the deficit was $6 billion. By contrast, the Clinton budget for fiscal 1996, which begins Oct. 1, [1995] proposes $1.6 trillion in spending against $1.4 trillion in revenues, and a deficit close to $200 billion.

In 2000, the last of the five years covered by that budget, spending is projected at $1.9 trillion, receipts at $1.7 trillion, and the deficit still about $200 billion. Those estimates, not surprising, have been rejected by the budget panels as they fashion their own plans.

Domenici says of the Clinton budget: "There is no deficit reduction of any significance." He says the Clinton plan would add $2 trillion to the national debt over the next five years, increasing each American's share of that debt to $26,000.

Recalling that Clinton's 1993–94 budget was described as a major deficit-reduction plan based on tax increases and spending cuts, Domenici said that the "nightmare" that he expected—higher taxes without deficit control—is coming to pass.

In the House, the budget resolution developed under Kasich would, by 2002, limit spending increases to estimated growth in revenue. Total revenues, now $1.4 trillion, are expected to reach $1.78 trillion by 2002, and spending would equal the latter amount.

Although such balance might sound like standard fiscal policy, it would be a departure for the federal government. Since 1950, there have been five budget surpluses totaling $16.9 billion and 40 budget deficits totaling $4.5 trillion. The last surplus was in 1969.

A preliminary House plan forecast total spending for the seven fiscal years 1996–2002 at $11.7 trillion, compared with $9.5 billion over the previous seven years. The key change is capping outlays at income levels. Under longstanding federal budget policy, spending is set by the assumed growth of programs. If the total cost of that growth exceeds the increase in revenues, the gap is covered by federal borrowing, which reached a record $290 billion in fiscal 1992.

The balanced-budget amendment remains the principal GOP initiative on curbing spending.

The movement for constitutional change, rather than a law subject to revision and repeal by a majority vote in Congress, stemmed from the failure of the various mandates setting legislative targets and timetables, most notably the 1985 Gramm-Rudman-Hollings measure calling for a balanced budget by 1990.

(The term "majority" can be overstated. Half of the members of each house can comprise a quorum to do business in their respective chambers, and a majority of a quorum—or 26 senators and 110 representatives—can pass measures that include the modification or repeal of legislatively set budget restraints. It would take the votes of a two-thirds majority of each house, however—67 senators and 290 representatives—as well as the consent of 38 state legislatures to approve a constitutional amendment mandating a balanced federal budget.)

While opponents of a balanced-budget amendment—most of them Democrats—argue that budget balance is simply a matter of congressional will, advocates say the long cycle of imposing and abandoning fiscal restraint demonstrates the need for an irrevocable mandate.

After passing the House 300-132, the balanced-budget amendment fell in the Senate, 66-34. Senate Majority Leader Bob Dole, R-Kan., plans another vote when, he says, he has won over that last vote needed to send the proposal to the states for ratification or when he feels it will cause maximum political damage to the 33 Democrats who voted against it. (The 34th negative vote came from Republican Sen. Mark O. Hatfield of Oregon.)

With polls showing that a substantial majority of Americans support a balanced-budget amendment, Dole has suggested that another vote testing the Democratic position might come just before the 1996 election if a 67th vote for it has not been found sooner.

Much of the immediate and long-term action on the budget—as well as pressure for the amendment—is being driven by the recognition, which has become bipartisan, that fiscal trends of the recent past cannot be sustained without severe damage to the economy.

Without a course correction, those trends will lead to "inescapable and staggering" results, says Rep. Henry J. Hyde, R-Ill., chairman of the House Judiciary Committee and chief House strategist on the balanced-budget amendment. He points to unending deficits that will eventually require debt-service payments equal to 40 percent of all federal spending.

When that happens, he asks, "where will we find the money for essential government services and programs? . . . How will the private sector finance business start-ups—job creation—with debt service eating up almost half of the private investment funds generated each year?"

The 1994 election victory that gave control of Congress to Republicans running on anti-tax, anti-spending platforms has had major impacts on the fiscal debates and budget politics. It has eliminated any prospect of tax increases as a deficit-reduction device and has made spending restraint a highly desirable policy for members of Congress contemplating re-election bids.

An indication of the changed environment is the extent to which some Democrats long opposed to the line-item veto now support it. By large margins in both houses, Congress has approved this form of veto, which lets the president reject individual items, such as pork-barrel projects, in big spending bills he previously had to sign or veto in their entirety.

To be sure, there is concern about the budget problem on both sides of the aisle. Sen. Bill Bradley, D-N.J., a fiscal-policy authority for his party, says the first call on federal tax collections "is not defending the nation or feeding children or providing for education or building highways or sending money to Social Security recipients. The first place that money has to be spent is to pay those bondholders who have loaned us money."

Such comments are being made with greater frequency and intensity amid growing awareness of the consequences of unchecked deficit spending on both domestic programs and the nation's need to remain competitive in world trade. U.S. failure to cope with red-ink finances is cited as an important factor in the recent sharp decline of the dollar in world markets.

Many advocates of a balanced budget say that the problem is brought into its sharpest focus through a calculation offered by the Concord Coalition, a private, bipartisan group committed to eliminating the deficit. This group notes that "the national debt of the United States increases $9,600 each second, $576,000 each minute, $34,560,000 each hour, and $829,440,000 each day."

## BALANCING THE FEDERAL BUDGET[3]

Proposals to amend the U.S. Constitution to require a balanced federal budget have been before Congress for the last

[3]Article from *Congressional Digest* 74/2:33 F '95. Copyright © 1995 by The Congressional Digest Corporation. Reprinted with permission.

60 years, but none has ever passed. Today, however, with persistently high federal deficits and a new Republican majority in Congress, the amendment has moved to the forefront of the national agenda.

The main reason for the current surge of support for a balanced budget amendment is the state of the federal budget itself. The federal deficit—the amount by which government outlays exceed receipts in a given fiscal year—while declining slightly over the last two years, was $203 billion in 1994. The Congressional Budget Office [CBO] projects that the deficit will drop to $176 billion in 1995, but rise again to $322 billion (with inflation) by 2002. Meanwhile, the national debt—the cumulative amount that the government has borrowed to meet its obligations—was $4.7 trillion in 1994. To put these numbers in perspective, twenty years ago the federal deficit was $6.1 billion, and the federal debt stood at $484 billion.

The balanced budget constitutional amendment is a top priority of the new Republican leadership in Congress. The *Contract With America,* a document signed by Republican congressional candidates prior to the November 1994 elections, promised a floor vote on the amendment within the first hundred days of the new Congress.

Article V of the U.S. Constitution outlines the procedure for consideration of a constitutional amendment: A joint resolution must be approved by a two-thirds vote in both the House and Senate, after which the proposal must be ratified by three-fourths of the States.

While there is broad general support for a balanced budget amendment, questions remain regarding the specific provisions. The basic language now under consideration requires the Federal budget to be balanced by 2002, or the second year after the amendment has been ratified by the States, whichever is later. The requirement could be waived in times of military engagement.

The House version of the legislation also stipulates that taxes could not be increased without approval by three-fifths of both the House and Senate. So far, drafters of the legislation have not been able to reach a consensus on this issue, with many fearing that tax revenues might be so broadly defined as to encompass changes in Medicare and tariffs, for example. Other unresolved issues include whether the amendment might shift the fiscal burden of federal programs to state and local governments, and whether certain budget categories, such as Social Security, should be exempt.

In the meantime, supporters of a balanced budget constitutional amendment state that they have lost faith in the ability of Congress to bring federal spending down to an acceptable level through statutory means. They also maintain that one of the fundamental principles recognized by the Founding Fathers was that government should not go into debt, saddling future generations with the burden of current expenditures—and that the lack of a balanced budget provision in the Constitution is an omission that should be corrected. They argue further that if the budget is not brought under control, deficit spending will grow progressively worse, and the nation will be unable to meet its responsibilities in such important areas as national defense or Social Security payments to future retirees.

Opponents, on the other hand, believe that a balanced budget amendment represents an easy substitute for confronting difficult choices and working for more efficient and accountable government—and an approach that ultimately would prove ineffective and perhaps even unenforceable. They argue that matters of fiscal policy, which tend to fluctuate with economic conditions, do not belong in the Constitution—a permanent document that sets forth ideals and rights and the fundamental structure of government. They also fear that economic disruption could result from sudden reductions in government programs that affect the health and well-being of citizens.

If a balanced budget amendment does pass the Congress, the attention—and the debate—will shift to the states, which will have seven years in which to approve or disapprove this fundamental change in how the federal government manages the taxpayers' money.

## UNBALANCING THE ECONOMY[4]

It's rare that one roots for the Senate—a body designed to limit democracy in the interests of the privileged—to block something, but in the case of the balanced budget amendment, you've got to hope the upper house can summon all its obstructive powers. If adopted, the B.B.A. [Balanced Budget Amendment]

[4]Article from *The Nation* magazine 260/10:329, 331+ Mr 13 '95. Copyright © 1995 by The Nation Company, L. P. Reprinted with permission.

would force unimaginably deep cuts in federal spending and would almost certainly increase the risk of an ordinary recession turning into a deep, protracted collapse.

Passed by the House on January 26, [1995] the B.B.A. would require the President to submit, and Congress to adopt, a budget in which projected revenues equal or exceed expenditures. This requirement could be waived during war or in "an imminent and serious military threat to national security," or in peacetime by a three-fifths vote of both houses of Congress.

Legally, the amendment is murky. It's not clear what would happen if Congress ignored its strictures. Would the Chief Justice become a kind of bankruptcy judge, and run the government as if it were a firm in receivership?

Economically, the B.B.A. is terrifying. Suppose we enter a recession, as we do every three or four years, and an unplanned deficit materializes. In a slump, revenues sag, as employment and profits shrink, and expenses mount, as people file for public benefits. Historically, automatic expansion of the deficit has acted as a stabilizer, preventing the economy from entering a 1930s-style tailspin. But under the B.B.A., Congress would be forced either to cut spending or raise taxes the moment red ink appeared on the federal ledger. We'd replace stabilizers with destabilizers. Of course, 60 percent of Congress could vote to waive the B.B.A., but that seems unlikely in the present political environment, and besides, given the lags and imperfections in our data-gathering machinery, appropriate action may come too late.

That's only the beginning of the problem. Let's not even worry about recessions turning into depressions, and just review the math. Congressional Republicans have pledged to exempt Social Security and the Pentagon from any cuts, and only a revolutionary government would dare touch interest payments on outstanding debts. Those sacred cows account for more than half of federal expenditures, meaning that all other spending would have to be cut by one-quarter. Or, all spending on the following could be eliminated: foreign aid, science (including space), energy, natural resources and the environment, agriculture, transportation, community and regional development, education and training. Admittedly there are many abominations hidden in these categories—nature-killing boondoggles disguised as "reclamation," support for murderous regimes, austerity programs disguised as foreign aid. But the fiscal equivalent of group punishment would guarantee a slaughter of the innocents along with the guilty.

Support for the B.B.A. is driven by the feeling that the federal government is growing. In fact, it's not. As a share of G.D.P., Washington's spending is lower than it was in 1983, and Clinton's own budget—which has to be seen as an upper limit—projects that by the year 2000 it will be back to 1968 levels. As a share of the population, the federal civilian work force is lower than it has been since 1941, and as a share of total employment, it's the smallest since 1934. For all levels of government combined, U.S. public spending is the lowest of any rich industrial country, and our deficit is the smallest (tied with Japan's) of the Group of Seven. Since this stinginess doesn't seem to make for a healthy economy or a happy populace, it's hard to see why even more would do the trick.

Not that deficits are a good habit over the long term. Instead of taxing rich people, the government borrows from them, and pays them more than $200 billion a year in interest for the privilege. We could eliminate the deficit in all but recession years by another round of income tax increases on the richest one percent and by eliminating their precious tax breaks. But that's the last thing on the minds of the B.B.A.'s sponsors. And from the looks of Clinton's budget, it appears to be the last on his as well.

## NO COURAGE TO CUT[5]

The U.S. Constitution is a carefully balanced document, calculated, in the words of an 18th-century politician, "to secure the personal rights of the people so far as declarations on paper can effect the purpose, leaving unimpaired the great powers of the government." The rights of the people and the powers of the government are again at stake as Congress moves quickly to push through a balanced-budget amendment. The claim that the U.S. government should spend only as much as it makes—an economic theory rarely practiced by businesses or households—has been on the legislative table since 1986. Now, under a Republican majority, the balanced-budget amendment is all but certain to be approved and sent to the states for final ratification.

Before that happens, the American public would do well to

[5]Article by James M. Wall from *The Christian Century* 112/3:75–6 J 25 '95. Copyright © 1995 by Christian Century Foundation. Reprinted with permission.

stop for a moment and consider the implications. An economic theory designed to negate the Keynesian notion that an unbalanced budget can, under some circumstances, be beneficial to a democracy has no business being part of the Constitution. Social engineering from the political right is basically the same as social engineering from the political left: it's the passage into law of theories of human behavior. It is common for a congressional majority to act to implement its theories; congressional liberals have been doing so for decades. However, legislative action, not a constitutional amendment, is the appropriate forum for such efforts.

Many economists contend that today's economic situation calls for reduction in spending and increased revenues, but circumstances could change. There may be times, as John Maynard Keynes argued, when heavy government spending is required to stimulate the economy. There is nothing sacred about deficit spending, just as there is nothing sacred about a balanced budget. To amend the nation's central guiding document to implement a prevailing economic theory makes as much sense as implementing an amendment that constitutionally imposes a particular moral view on the use of alcohol—which in fact Americans decided to do through the 18th Amendment, adopted in large measure because Protestants resented the drinking habits of immigrants, most of whom were Catholics. The consequences were disastrous.

The belief that Demon Rum was immoral, and should therefore be illegal, was a conviction soon outvoted when the drinking population became strong enough to outvote the nondrinkers. After a few years of social turmoil, the 21st Amendment was adopted to overturn Prohibition. This decision was reached when it became apparent to a sufficient majority that a moral theory held by only one segment of the population—even a majority segment—does not belong in the Constitution.

While a moral case can still be made that beverage alcohol does far more harm than good, and that its absence would—in the long run—be a blessing to the population, that case is best made by a legislative majority, not by a constitutional amendment. It is the purpose of legislation to implement the will of a ruling majority; it is the purpose of the judiciary to determine whether or not congressional action has violated the Constitution. When the people confuse the shifting winds of legislative will with the bedrock principles of the Constitution, it's unsettling for the republic.

Instead of voting to curb spending and move toward a balanced budget through legislative action, the current Congress is apparently prepared to hide behind a constitutional amendment. The Republican strategy to pass the amendment through Congress and gain ratification in the necessary 38 states has contained two elements that make it clear that the amendment is designed to eliminate or reduce federal programs which the Congress lacks the political will and courage to toss out on its own.

One provision is a requirement that Congress may not raise taxes without a three-fifths majority in both houses—an almost impossible vote without evidence of a national emergency. The second provision that makes it obvious that legislators are hiding behind the skirts of a constitutional amendment is the promise to state governments that the federal government will not require that states assume any unfunded programs. In effect, the proposed amendment states that the federal budget must be balanced by the year 2002. Reaching that target date would almost certainly entail dismantling federal programs developed under Democratic congressional leadership since World War II.

The 1994 election was clearly a mandate—at least from those citizens who chose to vote (less than a majority)—indicating that the public wanted less government and fewer taxes. One public opinion poll found that as many as 80 percent of the public agrees that this goal could be accomplished through a balanced budget. What the poll does not reveal is the strength of that desire when coupled with actual programs to be cut or eliminated. If Social Security and military spending are exempted, as the Republican majority promises, that leaves the rest of the federal budget, which contains programs that benefit distinct segments of the population, none of whose advocates can be expected to voluntarily walk the plank for extermination.

Mining subsidies in the West, college loans for the middle class, tax breaks for corporations, housing subsidies, the space program, foreign aid, crime prevention programs, support for the homeless, children and families, support for public radio and television, the arts, and even the congressional historian are but a few of the expenditures certain to rally political clout to avoid cuts. The Republican majority knows this, which is why, rather than ask Congress to cut programs to achieve a balanced budget, it is adopting the strategy of an amendment to force cuts by the year 2002.

Assume for the moment that the amendment gets its necessary congressional and individual state support and becomes part of the Constitution. A balanced federal budget would then cease to be this year's political rhetoric expounding an economic theory, and would become a national policy as firm as those that guaranteed equal rights for racial minorities and voting rights for women. And then assume that by 2002, seven years into the future, the Congress still has not displayed the political will to cut programs or raise taxes—a reasonable assumption, even under a mandated deadline. If the amendment becomes part of the Constitution, the U.S. Supreme Court would assume the role of national legislator, dictating to Congress which programs it would cut or eliminate and how much revenue it would have to raise to achieve a balanced budget.

What the Congress lacks the courage or will to do now, it will, in effect, turn over to the Supreme Court to do in the year 2002. If one happens to believe that a balanced federal budget is as central to the well-being of the American people as, say, the elimination of slavery, then let the amendment go forward. But if one cherishes the careful balance between rights and powers inherent in our Constitution, the passage of this amendment makes about as much sense as the passage of the Prohibition amendment. It is right and proper for Congress to put carefully considered theories into legislative action; it is a serious mistake to rely on the Supreme Court of 2002 to do what Congress lacks the courage to do itself.

---

## ATTENTION, DEFICIT DISORDER[6]

Remember the deficit? Back during the 1992 election, a consensus held that its unchecked expansion was sapping the nation's economic vigor. Ross Perot got 19 percent of the vote running on the issue; Bill Clinton made it the highest domestic priority of his first year. At heavy political cost, the administration passed a plan to tame it with a mix of tax increases and spending cuts. As a result, the projected budget shortfall for 1995 fell from nearly

[6]Article by Jacob Weisberg from *New York* Magazine 28:36-7 Ja 2 '95. Copyright © 1995 K-III Magazine Corporation. All rights reserved. Printed with permission.

$300 billion to $162 billion, according to the latest figures. That drop was at least partly responsible for lower interest rates in 1993 that lasted through the first half of 1994, and helps explain the endurance and vitality of the present recovery.

Deficit reduction was the central good deed of Clinton's first term. The job, however, isn't finished: The deficit rises again in 1996, and will be $397 billion by the year 2004, according to the Congressional Budget Office [CBO] estimate. As a result of deficits past, the national debt is fast approaching $5 trillion, and interest on it eats 16 percent of federal revenues. Yet since the November elections, the issue has virtually disappeared. Both parties still propose to cut spending. But both the $76-billion plan Clinton announced last week and the $176-billion Republican version would forgo serious deficit reduction in favor of a middle-class tax cut of dubious large-scale economic value.

Even more depressing from the viewpoint of those who think the deficit matters is the collapse of the Kerrey Commission. Give Bob Kerrey, the free-thinking Nebraskan, credit for courage. Kerrey asked for a presidential panel on entitlement spending as his reward for casting the deciding vote in favor of the president's controversial 1993 budget. In the middle of his own re-election bid, he raised the only public issue more incendiary than onanism: cutting Social Security. And he did this because, like everyone else who has studied the issue, he understands there can be no long-term cure for deficit spending without cutting programs that benefit the middle and upper classes.

The American Association of Retired Persons [AARP] ministry of information will be quick to point out that Social Security does not contribute to the deficit, that its surpluses actually make the government's excess of expenditures over receipts appear smaller than it is. But as the baby-boom generation approaches retirement and life expectancy rises, the program's over-the-top generosity—most current retirees will receive more than double the value of what they paid in—becomes an enormous unfunded liability. And because the Social Security—funding FICA [Federal Insurance Contributions Act] is one of the most regressive taxes ever leveled—a flat 12.4 percent on everyone's first dollar of income—raising it is no option.

As the Kerrey Commission discovered, Medicare is an even more urgent problem. Like Social Security, the program is a Ponzi-esque intergenerational transfer of wealth; it is paid for by current workers via a burdensome payroll tax, yet provides a level of benefits that cannot be sustained. Medicare will devour 13 percent of next year's federal revenues, about four times the amount spent on welfare and food stamps. Thanks to rising costs and increasing longevity, Medicare's share will balloon to 20 percent of the budget in ten years. The cost of Medicaid and federal pensions is exploding as well. According to the Kerrey Commission's findings, "In 2012, unless appropriate policy changes are made in the interim, projected outlays for entitlements and interest on the national debt will consume all tax revenues collected by the federal government."

Kerrey and his vice-chairman, the retiring moderate Republican John Danforth of Missouri, struggled in vain for consensus on how to address this coming crisis. Among the solutions Kerrey considers most palatable are gradually increasing the retirement age to seventy, means-testing Medicare benefits, and adjusting the consumer price index. But to no avail; eight members of the commission (including, interestingly enough, Kerrey's mentor, Pat Moynihan) declined to sign even the milquetoast statement contained in a December 15, [1995] admission-of-failure letter to the president. "In the end, you have to be willing to give up your political career to get meaningful deficit reduction," Kerrey says. Few were. His recommendations were not so much disputed as ignored, and the man dismissed as a dreamer. This response was abetted by an election in which entitlement reform was disavowed by both parties. Since November 8, [1995] Newt Gingrich has repeated that Social Security is "off the table." Clinton has gone him one better, promising not to touch a hair on the head of Medicare either.

It's a situation that makes the oft-mocked balanced-budget amendment look almost appetizing. This proposal is one of the central pieces of Republican dogma—item No. 1 in the *Contract With America*. But that doesn't prove it's a bad idea. There's certainly reason to be skeptical of the Republicans' bona fides on the issue; in the past, they have supported the amendment instead of proposing a real balanced budget, while the Democrats have at least taken the first steps toward sobriety. Still, it might make sense for the Democrats, for substantive and political reasons, to embrace the cause.

Liberal-minded critics of the amendment do raise some valid objections. An amendment would foreclose the use of Keynesian fiscal stimulus, running temporary deficits as needed, to jump-start the economy in a recession. An amendment would be largely unenforceable and easy to evade: According to all versions, Congress can excuse itself by a three-fifths vote. Moreover, an amendment might breed a culture in which "dynamic scoring" and other phony accounting methods would be used to secure technical compliance. Robert Reischauer, the saintly director of the Congressional Budget Office, who is about to be offed by the Newtoids, worries that Congress might balance the budget through subterranean mandates on the private sector and local government. He also points out that there's nothing wrong in theory with running a deficit for purposes of investment, as opposed to current consumption. And finally, it is unfortunate to blithely tinker with what Madison and Hamilton wrought.

All true enough. But the point about a constitutional amendment isn't that it would miraculously balance the budget. It's that it would focus the mind, forcing choices that are now being wished away. In this sense, the balanced-budget amendment is a kind of souped-up version of the Gramm-Rudman-Hollings Act of 1985, which threatened across-the-board cuts if deficit targets weren't met. The targets were deferred, and part of the law was declared unconstitutional. But Gramm-Rudman served as a lever to force the kind of deficit reduction that would never have happened in its absence. And for the programs Democrats care about, an amendment means fairer cuts. Otherwise, it is likely Republicans will slash exclusively at what's left of nondefense discretionary spending (i.e., the poor), while demagogically leaving middle- and upper-class entitlements alone.

Democrats should be wary, however, of what Republicans mean when they use the words *balanced-budget amendment*. The version in the GOP contract, which will soon make its way through Henry Hyde's Judiciary Committee, requires a supermajority of three fifths for any tax increase. This not only has nothing to do with balancing the budget, it would prevent it. Many needed cuts— like increasing Medicare premiums for the well-to-do and subjecting various benefits to taxation—would be forbidden because they are, strictly speaking, tax increases. The version sponsored by Illinois senator Paul Simon, on the other hand, plays it straight, leaving Congress all its options. The Simon bill could be strengthened by borrowing an idea from Reischauer (who says he would support the amendment only as an act of desperation): Insert a "poison pill," so that the amendment repeals itself automatically after two consecutive balanced budgets.

Politically, it makes little sense for the administration to continue to object even to the *notion* of a balanced-budget amendment. Clinton has done the heavy lifting on deficit reduction thus far and paid a price for it. Meanwhile, the Republicans, who inflated the deficit in the first place under Presidents Reagan and Bush, are poised to take credit for abolishing it while in reality deferring the problem until at least 2002, the soonest an amendment could take effect. By endorsing a better version of the plan, the administration would deprive the GOP of one of its best issues for 1996. Even if one assumes quick passage by the required thirty-eight states, Clinton will be long gone by the time it kicks in. Given the huge deficit the Reaganites left on the welcome mat for him, it seems only appropriate to let the next Republican president finish cleaning up the mess.

# III. CUTTING ENTITLEMENTS

## EDITOR'S INTRODUCTION

Undoubtedly, the riskiest, political aspect of balancing the budget lies in the area of entitlements. But, in order to balance a budget in severe deficit, ways to cut government spending must be found. One way—some observers say the only way—involves budget cuts that affect a variety of social programs, known as entitlements, which include, welfare, Social Security, veterans benefits, unemployment benefits, food stamps, Medicare, and public housing—in other words, programs that affect large segments of the American public. As the budget knife approaches these programs, public interest lobbying groups, such as the American Association of Retired People (AARP), voice their concerns.

The first article, "To Cut or Not to Cut," from *Modern Maturity*, analyzes the real expenditures associated with certain programs like Social Security and Medicare. Hoopes cites a discovery by the AARP that while the budget deficit has nearly doubled since the 1970s as a percentage of gross domestic product, entitlement spending has remained stable. The AARP contends that Social Security is a self-financing program that has begun to replace loss of revenue from the 1981 tax cuts and a bloated defense program as the favorite scapegoat in the budget deficit.

"Clinton's Medicare Cuts . . . ," by Judy Licht from *Ms.* insists that as cuts in Medicare and Social Security loom, particular groups like elderly women, suffer a greater share of the burden than other groups. Licht calls for a lowering of Medicare premiums and payments to offset the cutting of medical benefits.

From *USA Today*, an article by Willard Hogeboom entitled "Social Security: Sacred Cow of Entitlement Programs" discusses the reasons behind political reluctance to cut Social Security benefits. The slashing of social aid causes a hostile reaction among the groups most affected, with the political result being felt in the form of lost votes and endorsements. The author quotes, Tip O'Neill's phrase "Social Security is the third rail of politics. Touch it and you die!"

Peter G. Peterson, a highly respected economist, co-founder of the Concord Coalition, and a member of Clinton's bi-partisan committee on entitlement reform, discusses the problems of coping with entitlement costs in his speech, "Entitlement Reform: A Key to America's Future." Programs like Social Security are already overburdened and have, according to Peterson, $7 trillion in unfunded liabilities. The prospect is made worse by the fact that the largest generation of Americans, the Baby-Boomers, will soon constitute the largest group of senior citizens this country has ever known.

In the final article of this section, Robert J. Bresler, in "Facing the Painful Truth: The 1995 Budget Debates," maintains that because most mandatory spending programs are not means-tested, it is the middle class and not the poor who are the beneficiaries. If the budget is ever to be balanced, many Americans, he states "will have to see their subsidies, benefit checks, or low-interest loans reduced or eliminated."

---

## TO CUT OR NOT TO CUT[1]

The word "entitlements" has recently taken on a sinister connotation, but what does it really refer to in the federal budget?

There are up to 400 entitlement programs falling into four categories: (1) pension and disability—primarily Social Security, military and civilian retirement, and veterans' pensions—$385 billion in Fiscal Year 1993; (2) health care—primarily Medicare and Medicaid, but including veteran and federal employee health benefits—$230 billion in FY '93; (3) "safety nets"—unemployment compensation, family support, food stamps, etc.—$120 billion in FY '93; (4) others—the largest of which are the agricultural programs—totaling just over $30 billion in FY '93.

There are also many programs known as "tax expenditures," or "tax entitlements," that give benefits to anyone who qualifies. The largest are the exclusion for pension-plan contributions, the exclusion of employer-provided contributions for health insurance, and the home-mortgage-interest deduction. Together,

[1]Article by Roy Hoopes from *Modern Maturity* 37/6:10–1 N '94. Reprinted with permission from *Modern Maturity*. Copyright © 1994, American Association of Retired Persons.

these cost the government about $400 billion in FY '93—a figure
that's doubled since 1980 and is still growing.

Entitlements have been part of federal spending and tax policy for more than fifty years. Some now say they are the main
cause of the annual deficit and the spiraling national debt. But
entitlements did *not* produce these. The national debt, which
climbed from $645 billion at the end of 1979 to $4.6 trillion today,
resulted from the loss of federal revenues (some since restored)
produced by ERTA—the Reagan Economic Recovery Tax Act of
1981—from huge defense expenditures (gradually being reduced), the high interest rates at the time of debt financing, and,
for a while, the savings-and-loan bailout. ERTA was part 1 of a
two-part "Reagan Revolution," Reagan Budget Director David
Stockman's term for their economic program. Part 2 was to comprise massive cuts in federal spending, but Stockman, Reagan and
the Congress were unable to bring them about. The result, Stockman said later, was "an unintended exercise in free-lunch economics."

As John Gist and Kristen Aleksa of AARP's Public Policy Institute point out in *Entitlements & the Federal Budget Deficit: Setting the
Record Straight,* the budget deficit nearly doubled from 2.4 percent of the gross domestic product in the 1970s to 4.7 percent in
the early 1990s, while entitlement spending remained stable, av-
eraging about 11 percent from 1975 through 1993. During that
period, the primary cause of the growth in deficits was the massive 1981 tax cuts.

"This lost revenue," AARP's study shows, "would have eliminated about two-thirds of the debt we have accumulated since
1982." The study challenges similar myths that have grown up
around entitlements:

*Medicare and Medicaid are mainly responsible for increasing nation-
al health costs.* Although Medicare has been cut several times in
recent years, the increasing costs of the government health programs are part of the overall national health-care crisis that any
health-care-reform plan that's enacted must resolve (if we are
ever to get the deficit under control).

*Social insurance programs mainly benefit the affluent.* In fact, nearly 75 percent of Social Security and Medicare benefits go to
households with incomes other than Social Security under
$20,000 a year, less than 2 percent to those with over $100,000.

*Middle-class entitlements are "out of control."* Actually, since 1985
the growth of both Social Security and Medicare has slowed dra-

matically—Social Security by 2.4 percent a year, Medicare by 5.4 percent. (Both figures adjusted for inflation.)

Another popular myth is that Social Security recipients get back all the money they put in within three years. This may have been true early on, but today it will take the average worker retiring at 65 about twelve years to recover his or her contributions.

AARP contends that Social Security should not even be part of the entitlements debate, agreeing with former U.S. Commissioner on Aging William D. Bechill that "we need to be figuratively screaming from the housetops that Social Security is a self-financed program, has a huge budget surplus, and is currently financed to assure payments of benefits through the year 2036 . . . ." Although the time frame is now 2029—some years after the Baby Boomers have begun retiring—this gives us, most experts agree, plenty of time to make it fiscally sound again for the long term.

After it became clear that without remedial action the 1981 tax cuts would produce endless deficits, arguments for restructuring the nation's financial position began to appear. But as time passed, "entitlements" began to replace loss of revenue and huge defense spending as the primary scapegoats because several attempts to reduce the deficit were made (notably in 1990 and 1993) with limited success and defense spending is actually declining in real terms. In 1987 Peter G. Peterson, Richard Nixon's Secretary of Commerce and now a Wall Street banker, published a major article in *The Atlantic Monthly* [260: 43–50+ O '87], "The Morning After." He wrote that six years after the radical reforms of Reaganomics got under way, "Americans are about to wake up to reality." Although Peterson concluded that Reaganomics was "truly inexcusable," he said the problem was "interest costs and entitlement benefits unrelated to poverty (or to put it bluntly, welfare for the middle class and up)."

In 1993 Peterson's book *Facing Up* expanded on the same theme. And some of his ideas about entitlements were incorporated in the deficit-reducing proposals of the Concord Coalition—a body dedicated to eliminating the federal deficit. The Coalition, brainchild of Peterson and former Senators Warren Rudman (R-N.H.) and Paul Tsongas (D-Mass.), believes that entitlements are the main cause of the deficit. According to AARP studies, the Coalition's *The Zero Deficit Plan*, designed to eliminate the deficit early in the next century, is biased against the elderly and disabled, lacks a comprehensive program for containing health-care costs, seriously alters the earned-right concept of Social Security, and makes no significant cuts in defense spending or middle- and upper-income tax preferences. It does propose some tax increases, but they are mostly regressive consumption taxes that hurt low-income people most.

However, the Coalition has been able to elevate the concept of entitlement cutting as the solution to the deficit into the political mainstream. Last year [1993] Representative Marjorie Margolies-Mezvinsky (D-Penn.) promised she would vote for President Clinton's budget if he would appear at an entitlement-cutting conference she planned later.

Similarly, to persuade Senator Robert Kerrey (D-Neb.) to vote for his budget, the President agreed to appoint a Presidential Commission to discuss and recommend entitlement savings. The Bipartisan Commission on Entitlement and Tax Reform, chaired by Kerrey and Senator John Danforth (R-Mo.), comprises 32 members. On August 8, [1994] it issued its interim report; the final report to the President is due December 2, [1994] of this year. Its rules say 60 percent (twenty members) of the Commission must vote for a recommendation before it can be sent to the President. Kerrey said taxes were still on the table, although at the press conference after the interim report was released he said he was leaning toward an alternative tax structure—such as a consumption tax.

The interim report deliberately lacked specific recommendations. AARP agreed with the Commission's statements that Social Security and Medicare must be made sound for future generations and that rising health-care costs pose the most immediate problem; it faulted the Commission for not stressing that federal health-care spending is part of a system-wide problem.

As for the Commission's general mission, AARP legislative director John Rother says: "If we're going to talk about deficit reduction and sharing the burden, it must be remembered that entitlements go by and large to middle- and lower-income people. On the other hand, there are a lot of tax expenditures in the tax code that are skewed toward upper-income individuals. There will have to be equal scrutiny."

It's ironic that thirteen years and approximately $4 trillion later the entitlement-cutters are trying to enact part 2 of the Reagan Revolution—but without the Great Communicator's help in telling the American people why present and future seniors should bear the primary burden of correcting the "truly inexcusable" fiscal policy of the 1980s.

That his help is needed is dramatically confirmed by a July [1994] *Wall Street Journal*/NBC News poll showing that while 61 percent of those polled favored cutting entitlement programs, *66* percent were opposed to cutting Medicare, Social Security and Medicaid when they were specifically named among programs to be cut.

---

## CLINTON'S MEDICARE CUTS: THIS IS REALLY GOING TO HURT[2]

---

Julia Malberg is a seventy-six-year-old Maryland widow living on the edge of poverty. Her standard of living has dropped dramatically since the days when she raised six children on her husband's salary as a truck driver.

"Right now I don't buy a lot," she says. "I just wear what the kids hand me down, and I do without a lot of things I'd like to have." With only $674 a month in Social Security payments, Malberg, like most older women, has to ration her finances. "Because of the money" she hasn't had a complete physical in four years.

Though stories like Malberg's are far from unique, President Clinton targeted Medicare—the government "entitlement" program that provides health benefits to more than thirty million older citizens—when he needed money last summer [1992] to reduce the budget deficit.

Women will be hit hardest by the cuts. They generally live longer and poorer, outlasting men by seven years. Half the women in this country over 65 live on less than $8,189 a year. They have to stretch every dollar to pay their bills.

Clinton and Congress said they were only curbing the growth of Medicare. They said cutting $56 billion in Medicare spending over the next five years would have no direct impact on those who depend on these payments. Lobbyists for older people protested but then went back to their constituents and said things could be

[2]Article by Judith Licht from *Ms.* 4:90–2 N/D '93. Reprinted with permission of Ms. Magazine Copyright © 1993.

worse: an earlier deficit reduction proposal had called for $85 billion in cuts. So the lobbyists breathed a sigh of relief, patting themselves on the back for negotiating a better deal.

But this victory was short-lived. Within a month, details of Clinton's long-awaited health care reform program slipped out to the press: he planned to slash another $124 billion from Medicare to finance the health care reform package. Ironically, some seniors groups were sanguine about the proposal. Ardent supporters of deficit reduction, many members seemed concerned about their children and grandchildren, who could be hurt if the current leadership doesn't get a grip on skyrocketing costs. "The older generation believes very strongly in reducing the deficit and wants to do their share," says Patricia Smith, chief health lobbyist for the American Association of Retired Persons (AARP). Though the group has supported every deficit reduction bill in the last decade, it was ambivalent about this one.

The AARP leadership sat on the fence over the initial budget cuts, opposing them but not wanting to oppose the administration's deficit reduction bill. In the end, they thought it was more important that Clinton get his budget passed. "If this bill had not passed," says Smith, "there would not be much chance that we could move into health care reform."

It's already clear that the initial $56 billion in cuts will have a direct and negative impact on a select pocket of the population— the poorer recipients of Medicare. They will be paying more than they can afford and they may be getting fewer services from the medical community.

By viewing Medicare as a funding source for a national health plan, Clinton has put those who depend on Medicare in the middle of one of the toughest battles to come before Congress. Medicare recipients are key players in the debate over who will pay to provide health care for the thirty-seven million uninsured in this country. In essence, the government is robbing Peter (Medicare recipients) to pay Paul (the uninsured). "It seems ironic that in order to give access to everyone they take away access from older people and poorer people," says Charlotte Flynn, chair of the national board of the Gray Panthers, an anti-ageism activist group. Even so, the initial reaction of seniors groups to Clinton's health care reform package was to hold their fire. But unless older people mount an expensive and vocal campaign to protect their interests, their ability to pay their health bills and their access to decent medical care will be severely threatened.

Medicare is set up like a fee-for-service health insurance plan. The recipient pays a monthly premium, and the program usually pays 80 percent of the cost of doctors' visits, with a $100 annual deductible. This year the premium is $36.60 a month. As part of the $56 billion budget deficit reduction package, by 1998 the premium will rise to $62.20. That's almost a 70 percent increase, which may not severely affect older people who have higher incomes, but will make a big difference for women like Malberg. "I get along on small Social Security checks," she says. "That's all I have. If they keep dipping into that I don't know how they expect somebody like me to live."

Ruth Hodge will also be hurt. A seventy-four-year-old widow from Independence, Kansas, she worked until she was 65, first in a factory making radio parts and then in a publishing company putting together city directories. Today, all she has left is $530 a month in Social Security payments and $34 a year in interest from a small certificate of deposit.

If things get any tighter, Hodge says, "I'll probably have to give up my fresh fruits and vegetables."

Why should women like Ruth Hodge have to give up food to finance a national health care plan?

And if she doesn't pay, who will?

The fight over the health care package is going to be long and ugly. Special interests will spend millions of dollars on lobbying, and seniors advocates will have to be heard over the voices of other, very powerful interest groups, such as those for doctors, hospitals, and insurance companies.

For the most part, older activists believe that these interests are making astronomical profits and can afford to take a cut in income. As the Gray Panthers' Flynn says, "The only thing the insurance industry has done is to insure well people." The overarching belief that the health care system is flawed and that costs are out of control buoys some seniors groups in their support of Clinton's proposed plan. Medicare funds now grow at a rate of about 11 percent a year. The president wants to curb growth to a much lower rate, maybe 4 or 5 percent, and many seniors groups are willing to play ball for the sake of health care reform.

Many older persons, like Barbara Macdonald, coauthor (with Cynthia Rich) of *Look Me in the Eye: Old Women, Aging, and Ageism* (Spinsters Ink), supported Bill Clinton during the campaign. "With Clinton," she says, "you want to wait because he has vision and he has a sense of what the overall needs are." Older voters

saw in Clinton a willingness to change and an energy that was
missing under Reagan and Bush. But now that same energy,
"aimed like a laser" on cutting costs, is threatening, and many
seniors are treading lightly as Clinton unveils his new health care
program. "Older people are very uneasy about fighting with the
younger generation," Macdonald says, "until it is very clear what
the issue is going to be."

In Washington, D.C., the lobbyists have been slow to come out
against the $124 billion in additional Medicare cuts. There's talk
around Capitol Hill that seniors groups didn't fight hard enough
to stop the initial $56 billion cut. There's a sense that they let their
poorer constituents down because they didn't emphasize that the
people who cannot afford to pay more—a disproportionate number of whom are women—are in fact going to have to pay more.

Seniors, for the most part, favor universal health insurance
coverage, and they are willing to make some sacrifices so they
won't be perceived as a burden on the younger population. "The
old do not want to be a stumbling block to prevent a national
single-payer system," says Macdonald. "They're looking at the
common good, but when it comes down to the line, believe me,
you'll hear from them."

Former New York Congresswoman Bella Abzug thinks it's not
a moment too soon for seniors organizations to start raising their
voices. She warns that they are "making a big mistake" by not
fighting the proposed cuts. "They've got themselves in a bind,"
she says. "They settled for less" when they accepted the $56 bil-
lion cut without putting up too much of a fight. She's afraid that if
any more is cut there is no guarantee that Clinton will be able to
live up to his promises to provide long-term care and prescription
drug benefits. Instead, older people may find that there is not
enough money in Medicare to cover their needs and there will be
a disincentive for doctors to treat them.

The angriest voices coming from the [former] Congress are
those of two Democrats from California, Henry Waxman and Pete
Stark, who agree that seniors will suffer under the cuts.

If the president succeeds in curbing the growth of Medicare,
older people could ultimately benefit, but only if the savings are
passed on to them through lowering both their Medicare premiums and their payments.

Clinton is also promising to use some of the program's estimated savings for prescription drug plans and long-term benefits
that are not now covered under Medicare.

But there is a downside. And a risk. Older persons could be hoping for savings that will never be realized. All the costs are projections, and how the program unfolds after negotiations that some say will take at least a year is unknown.

Seniors could also be supporting a plan that will discriminate against them in the long run. If, for example, the package puts a cap on the amount a doctor or hospital can charge a Medicare patient but does not put the same restriction on the rest of the population, doctors and hospitals might decide it's not worth it to treat Medicare recipients.

"Older people are often more complicated to treat because they have multiple conditions," says Marilyn Moon, a health economist at the Urban Institute, a think tank in Washington, D.C. If doctors are forced to charge $20, say, for an eighty-year-old woman who needs to spend thirty minutes with the doctor, as opposed to $30 for a twenty-year-old who needs ten minutes with the doctor, they might be less likely to accept the older patient.

Hospitals would also be getting paid less. Roughly 40 percent of the patients at St. Joseph's Mercy Hospital in Mount Clemens, Michigan, are on Medicare. The hospital now loses about 9.5 percent a year of what it costs to treat patients, according to Karen Ehrat, the chief operating officer. Further reductions mean the hospital will begin to scale back its services to Medicare patients.

With all this controversy over Medicare, why not just dismantle it and let Clinton's health care reforms care for the old? Dan Schulder of the National Council for Senior Citizens doubts that Medicare can stand alone as a separate system, as planned, once the reform package takes hold: "There will be inevitable conflicts in payment and quality standards between the two systems to the detriment of older persons."

Meanwhile, seniors are caught in a bad position. If there is no health care reform, they lose. Prices will definitely continue to skyrocket, and any illness that strikes women like Julia Malberg and Ruth Hodge will drown them in bills they can't pay. Yet if the reform package passes without clear financial protection for Medicare recipients who are in great need, then they also lose.

The special interests have already begun to fight: health insurance companies, doctors, and hospitals don't want to lower their profit margins. The tobacco and alcohol industries are fighting sin taxes. Some small business owners don't want to pick up more medical tabs, and lawyers don't want malpractice fees capped. The older persons' lobby, which is considered powerful and effective in Washington, can't afford to remain silent.

The risks are too great.

## SOCIAL SECURITY: SACRED COW OF ENTITLEMENT PROGRAMS[3]

In August, 1994, the Federal Bipartisan Commission on Entitlements and Tax Reform issued a preliminary report warning that government spending for entitlements—including Social Security, Medicare, Medicaid, and Unemployment Insurance—is growing at such a rapid rate that, unless Congress acts soon, it could bankrupt the country. The public has been hearing that message for some time now, but not paying heed to it.

While the possible bankruptcy of Federal entitlement programs is a very real prospect, there is another issue that needs to be addressed first. Politicians must start dealing honestly with the public about these programs, especially Social Security, in terms of what they are and what they are not.

Just before the 1994 elections, Federal Budget Director Alice Rivlin submitted a memo to President Clinton outlining a number of options of budget cuts to hold the deficit in check while allowing the administration to finance certain programs on its agenda. That memo was leaked to Republican leaders, who then accused the Clinton Administration of secretly planning to cut Social Security and Medicare. The President quickly gave public assurances that they would not be cut.

Once again, as so often in the past, Democrats and Republicans were united in a bipartisan public posture declaring Social Security and Medicare sacrosanct. It is this sort of charade that stands in the way of any serious attempt to address the problems of Social Security and Medicare.

The Social Security Act of 1935 included a broad spectrum of initiatives: old age assistance, federal-state public assistance, unemployment compensation, public health services, and vocational

[3]Article by Willard Hogeboom from *USA Today* 12–3 N '95. Copyright © 1995 by The Society for the Advancement of Education. Reprinted with permission.

rehabilitation. Most industrial countries of the world already had such legislation. The Franklin Roosevelt Administration knew that old-age assistance especially would face stiff opposition, so it was of critical importance that it not be seen as a welfare-type program. FDR [Franklin Delano Roosevelt] explained that those who participated could be "likened to the policyholders of a private insurance company."

A special payroll tax was created to support Social Security so that people would be aware of it every time they received their wages. The Federal Insurance Contributions Act (FICA) tax was labeled a contribution, like an insurance premium, and people knew they had to work a certain period of time to become eligible. Thus, every effort was made to make Americans believe that what was being deducted was "their money," which would earn interest and be paid back to them when they retired.

One of FDR's rationalizations for creating and presenting Social Security as he did was so that "no damn politician can ever scrap my Social Security program." He certainly succeeded. In the sixty years since its beginning, the mythology surrounding Social Security has become so entrenched that few politicians have dared criticize it, let alone try to scrap it. As former House Majority Leader Tip O'Neill once said, "Social Security is the third rail of politics. Touch it and you die!"

When the Republicans regained the White House in 1952, it was feared they would set about dismantling FDR's New Deal, including Social Security. That didn't happen. In the 1964 presidential campaign, Republican challenger Barry Goldwater brought up the issue: "I wanted to make Social Security solvent, to improve it. The first thing wrong with Social Security is the fact that it is compulsory. Secondly, it is not actuarially sound: it promises more benefits to more people than the incomes collected will provide." President Lyndon Johnson's camp promptly hung the "anti-Social Security" label on Goldwater, and he lost by a landslide.

During the 1982 Congressional election campaign, the Democrats attacked Republicans for the Reagan Administration's plans to reduce Social Security benefits, and the Republicans lost a considerable number of seats in the House. In 1986, the Democrats attacked Republicans for Reagan's plan to freeze Social Security cost of living adjustments, and the Republicans lost the Senate.

In 1983, responding to the fear that, when the baby boomers began to retire, there wouldn't be enough money to meet benefit

payments, the Reagan Administration introduced a series of
FICA tax increases to create a surplus. In 1989, six years and five
tax increases later, Sen. Daniel Patrick Moynihan (D.-N.Y.) blew
the whistle. He proposed canceling an upcoming FICA tax increase because the Bush Administration had been borrowing
from the surplus to offset skyrocketing Federal deficits. "Thiev-
ery" was the charge Moynihan leveled. Although his tax cut plan
didn't pass, Moynihan's action served to awaken many to how
Social Security really was operating.

During the six decades of Social Security, the myths created by
FDR have been perpetuated by each generation of politicians,
Democrat and Republican. For instance, there is the myth that it
is a form of social insurance to which members contribute
throughout their working lives, then draw upon at retirement—
but that is not the way the system really works. From the beginning, Social Security was a "pay-as-you-go" operation, as the money that was being paid in went right out in the form of benefits.
The fact is, Social Security is an intergenerational transfer of
money from workers to non-workers.

People paying Social Security tax have no property right to
that money, as they would have if it were an insurance policy or
retirement account. That was clearly spelled out in the 1960 U.S.
Supreme Court decision, *Flemming v. Nestor,* in which Justice John
Harlan wrote, "To engraft upon the Social Security system a concept of accrued property rights would deprive it of the flexibility
and boldness in adjusting to ever-changing conditions, which it
demands."

Nor is it the "sacred contract" that it often is described as.
That same Supreme Court decision affirmed that Congress
has the right "to alter, amend or repeal any part of the Social
Security Act."

Once Americans accept that what is paid in is a tax and not
*their* money, other myths automatically will be dispelled. For instance, people often compare the amount of money they paid in
FICA tax during their work years with the amount they receive in
benefits, as they would with an investment. However, it is not an
investment—it is a tax. Moreover, those who must pay income tax
on part of their benefits often claim they are being double-taxed
on the same money. Since it is not the same money, there is no
connection. In the *U.S. v. Lee,* the Supreme Court ruled that
FICA was "a true and independently justified tax, quite apart
from any linkage to the benefit program."

Another myth pertains to the so-called Trust Fund. As Goldwater pointed out, "there is no trust fund. It is a bookkeeping deception. The actual monies collected under the Social Security tax law go into the General Treasury of the United States." The Trust Fund contains nothing but IOUs from the federal government to itself.

The fundamental issue is one of demographics. As an intergenerational transfer of money from those who are working to those who are retired, there must be enough people employed to provide sufficient benefits. The large baby boom generation will be retiring after the turn of the century, when the numbers in the workforce will be declining. In 1950, there were sixteen workers for each individual receiving benefits. Today, there are just over three. By the end of the second decade of the 21st century, when the baby boomers are into retirement, there will be two workers for each recipient.

At the moment, entitlements constitute 54% of federal spending. Add to that the interest on the national debt, and the figure goes to 68%. By the year 2030, payments for entitlements and national debt interest will consume 100% of federal spending.

The Social Security Administration long has been monitoring what they call "projected trust fund exhaustion dates," when the Social Security and Medicare trust funds will be exhausted. Because of the great number of unpredictable factors involved, these are rough estimates and usually presented in a range from optimistic to pessimistic. What has been happening as time goes on is that the predicted exhaustion dates have been creeping back. In 1990, the pessimistic projection for the exhaustion of the Social Security fund was 2023. Now, it is 2014; for Medicare, 2000.

Senior citizens have the highest percentage of voters and are very protective of Social Security. Politicians warily remember when the Reagan Administration tried to cut benefits and the cost-of-living adjustment (COLA) during the 1980s.

Nevertheless, there is no shortage of proposals on how to address the problems of maintaining the funding to Social Security and Medicare. First, there is the means test, providing Social Security benefits only to those who can prove they need it. This answers the frequent criticism that many wealthy people collect Social Security. In reality, nearly 75% of benefits go to recipients whose annual income is less than $20,000; less than two percent is received by those with over $100,000 a year. To introduce a means test, though, would change the nature of the program to a form of welfare.

Second is increasing the tax on benefits. It already was increased greatly under the Clinton deficit reduction plan, and economists claim this has an adverse effect on economic growth.

A third idea is to increase the eligibility age. It already is going up to 67, and there is a limit on how far it can be raised.

Fourth are various suggestions on adjusting the COLA: skip a year; cap it; adjust it every other year; and raise it by dollar amounts, rather than percentages. This would affect all recipients, especially those in low-income groups, who would be hit hardest.

Finally, there is the "opt-out" proposal whereby workers could invest part of their contributions in alternative private investments. This presupposes a property right to contributions, which the Supreme Court has denied.

Discussion of possible solutions is fine and definitely is needed, but the first problem still is to get the politicians to be honest with the public on what Social Security is and is not. The public must bear part of this blame because it has not shown a desire to be dealt with honestly and openly. In the spring of 1994, the newsletter of the American Association of Retired Persons, the *AARP Bulletin,* ran an information piece on entitlements that included Social Security. This brought a flood of letters and phone calls from readers who objected to including Social Security among entitlements, which they took to be forms of welfare. The *Bulletin* then tried to explain how Social Security indeed *was* an entitlement, and this brought still more objections. Many readers simply did not want Social Security called an entitlement, even if it really was.

There are sixty years of mythology and misinformation to cut through before starting to "fix" Social Security. Catering to public misconceptions has become a monkey on the back of many politicians. The times of financial reckoning for many Social Security programs are almost upon the nation, but too many politicians believe these are issues for a future Congress and refuse to deal with them today. In the meantime, the gap between mythology and reality only will widen. There is a lot of re-educating that must be done, and that always is a lengthy process. Now is the time to begin.

## ENTITLEMENT REFORM: A KEY TO
## AMERICA'S ECONOMIC FUTURE[4]

I've been making speeches for longer than I care to remember. More often than not, I get the following response. I run into somebody on the street and they'll say, Mr. Peterson, that was a memorable speech you made. I used to be in the market research business, so I indiscreetly ask: "Really, what do you remember?" There's inevitably a long pause and, if they remember anything, it's some joke that I had told. So, I've evolved not the Peter Principle but the Peterson Principle, which is, if you're going to make a speech and you want anything to stick to the bone, tell a joke that is relevant to your message. So, today I have two jokes and I hope at least one of them sticks.

The first is the one that Ted Sorenson, President Kennedy's Assistant, has used in introducing me. He says,

"Peterson and I were on a trip to the Mideast. Shortly before the plane landed, two terrorists jumped out of their seats with machine guns and said, 'We're going to assassinate these two former public officials . . . on a bipartisan basis. We're going to give each of them their last wish.'" So they go to Peterson and say, "All right, what's your last wish, Peterson?" Peterson says, "I have one last speech I want to give on the relationship between entitlement spending and the deficit." The terrorists then turn to Sorenson and say, "All right, Sorenson, you've heard Peterson. What's your last wish?" Sorenson says, "In view of what you've heard from Peterson, my last wish is to be shot first."

My dreariness on this subject has even invaded The Blackstone Group where I work. We have an annual Christmas party in which the young professionals can express their unbridled hostilities to the partners. They play a game called Karnak that you may remember from Johnny Carson, in which they give the answers and you have to guess the questions. The answers at last year's Christmas party, shortly after my book came out, were 100,000, 99,999, one and zero. What were the questions? The questions were: "How many books did Peterson print?" "How many did he

    [4]Speech delivered to the Economic Club of Detroit, Detroit, Michigan by Peter G. Peterson, former Secretary of Commerce, on September 19, 1994 from *Vital Speeches of the Day* 61/9:272–6 F 15 '95. Copyright © 1994 by City News Publishing Co. Reprinted with permission.

sign and give away?" "How many were bought and paid for by someone else?" And, "How many were read?"

One speech for me is one too many. So, I'm going to spare you the long version of the book, or the speech, whatever. I'll just give you the basic theme of what's on my mind.

I argue that there are three imperatives. An economic imperative, a moral imperative, and a political imperative, if we're going to get our long-term act together and revitalize the American dream. To do that, we're going to have to increase productivity from its low levels. To do that, we're going to have to invest more. To do that, we're going to have to save more. And, to do that, we're going to have to *temporarily* consume less.

Now that inevitably gets back to the Sorenson joke—the relationship between entitlements and the deficit. The deficit has been consuming up to two-thirds of our all too shallow savings pool, and the deficit is very largely about consumption. The entitlements are almost all about consumption.

Now let me add the moral imperative. Now, I know what people think of investment bankers. It doesn't come very convincingly for an investment banker to be talking about morality. But I'll take a shot at it anyway.

I fell in love during the course of this book with the writings of a very elegant and moral American, Thomas Jefferson. And I was particularly impressed with some letters he wrote to James Madison. He wrote that if one generation incurred a public debt without paying it off, it was violating a natural and moral law. He reminded Madison that this country had fought a Revolutionary War over taxation without representation, and that every generation had an equal right to life, liberty and the pursuit of happiness. He argued, if one generation can charge another generation with its debt, then the earth would belong to the dead and not the living generation. He then went on to wonder whether if passing on a debt from one generation to another shouldn't be made unconstitutional. Now you can imagine what would happen to the financial markets today if such a law were passed with $4 trillion of debt.

Erich Banhoeffer, the German philosopher, put it differently: "The ultimate test of a moral society is the kind of world that it leaves to its children."

So, what are we leaving to our children? I don't want to depress you too relentlessly, but I do believe that the massive debts, the unprecedented unfunded liabilities and the unsustainable taxes that our own children and grandchildren will have to pay is nothing less than fiscal child abuse. I believe it is immoral in the sense that Jefferson was talking.

Let me give you but one number that relates to your grand-children and mine. If you read the President's budget report this year, you'll find a fascinating chapter called "Intergenerational Accounting." It was written by Larry Kotlikoff, a professor of economics at Boston University. What Larry has done is to take each generation's total net taxes—by which he means taxes after benefits received. For most of recent American history, your generation and mine has paid somewhere between 32 and 36 percent of their income in net taxes. It is his estimate that, if we are going to continue on our current path, it would require 82 percent of taxes of the current generation—the babies being born today—to pay off those debts.

Entitlement spending is driving this in the past and, as Ronald Reagan would say, "you ain't seen anything yet." But first, let's look historically. Entitlements in 1960 were 27 percent of the budget. They'll be about 60 percent in the year 2000, before the baby boomers retire.

Now, critics who want to protect the status quo say, "Well, our current debt problems are all a result of Reagan and Bush's de-fense budgets. I remind you that in the last 15 years or so, entitle-ments have grown three times faster than defense grew.

Then the AARP tells us that, "Well, it was those tax cuts that caused our problems." Wrong again. If you look at the total feder-al tax revenue percent of the GNP right now, you will find that between '86 and the year 2004, total taxes—which is the way I think you ought to look at it, including payroll taxes—are higher than the previous postwar taxes were. So, there's something else going on here called "spending in non-defense areas" that doesn't have anything to do with the common excuses—namely, defense spending and tax cuts.

I'm going to give you some projections and, when you hear them, you're going to say, "Why, those are unsustainable, they're unthinkable." But these are official estimates. Speaking of unsus-tainable, I was in the Nixon Administration, and we had a Repub-lican humorist—which I know many people consider an ultimate oxymoron—but we did, and his name was Herb Stein, Chairman of The Council of Economic Advisers. And Herb used to say to us: "If something is unsustainable, it tends to stop."

Now, another one, if you don't like that, is: "If your horse dies, I suggest you dismount."

A great deal of the numbers I'm going to give you are driven by demographic realities that have already occurred. Hayworth Robinson, a former chief actuary, the Chief of the Social Security Administration, tells me that 95 percent of the benefits for Social Security over the next fifty years will go to people that are already born. So, it's not a question of fancy demographic projections.

If you look over this time frame, here's the kind of an America that your children and grandchildren are going to be brought up in. Those over 65 will increase somewhere between 40 and 46 million. Just think of that! That's equivalent to adding another California and a whole new set of New England states to our population of elderly. The group will grow by somewhere between 125 and 145 percent. A particularly fast-growing group, of which I hope I become a member—namely, the over-85 group— is expected to grow 275 to 375 percent.

In my lifetime the U.S. used to have twenty-two children under the age of 5 for every person over the age of 85. During this time period, there is one official scenario that says that we will have more people over 85 than children under the age of 5. And we will look like a nation of Floridas.

If you look at who the taxpayers are, the working group, during the same period of time they're only going to grow by about 15 to 25 percent. So . . . the number of workers per retiree is changing dramatically.

In 1950, there were 16.5 covered workers for every Social Security beneficiary. Today, there are 3.2. In 2040 there will be about two. The effects of that, of course, are staggering when you think about the implications on payroll taxes that our kids and grandkids would be expected to pay.

If you go to Washington, you will now hear some ha-ha approaches to the unsustainable problem. They giggle and say, "Well, maybe we should annex Mexico. That'll take care of the problem." Or, I've heard another brilliant suggestion: "Why don't we require every family to have four children." I say to you, when Washington giggles, you better start crying.

Now, let's look to the future which is where the real problem is. The President's Bi-partisan Commission recently produced their statement of the problem. What is remarkable about this is that twenty Senators and Congressmen of both parties unanimously agreed on how serious the problem is. You tell me the last time twenty Senators and Congressmen agreed on anything. Of the eleven private members, ten of them supported the statement, and the only one who didn't was the President of the United Mine Workers.

Let me read to you what this official report says. "In the year 2012, unless appropriate changes are made, projected outlays for entitlements and interest on the debt will consume all of the tax revenues collected by the federal government. In 2030, projected spending for Medicare, Social Security and federal employment retirement programs alone, and Medicaid, will consume all of the tax revenues collected by the federal government. If all other federal programs, except interest on the national debt, grow no faster than the general economy, total federal outlays would exceed 37 percent of the economy. Today they are 22 percent of the economy. So, you're talking about adding 15 percent of the GNP, which is unthinkable, to the spending of this country."

Now, one of the common outs that people use is, they say, "Well, this is just a problem of the health care cost explosion. If we can just take care of that, without telling us how—the problem will be taken care of." That is demonstrably false. Let me read to you what our report says.

It says: "Even if the extraordinary increases in health care costs were eliminated after 1999, so that the cost for each person of a given age grew no faster than the economy, federal outlays for Medicare and Medicaid would double as a percentage of the economy by 2030. The aging of the population would drive combined Medicare, Medicaid and Social Security spending from about 8 percent of the economy to about 14 percent of the economy." This assumes you get health care costs under control, which I would say is a most generous assumption, to put it gently.

Now, what are the effects of these future entitlement costs on the annual budget deficit? The protectors of the status quo tell us that the Social Security retirement system is in "surplus." That, of course, doesn't include Medicare, which is part of the total Social Security payroll system. "Therefore," they say, "Social Security is not part of the problem." But what they don't tell us is about the future outlook on Social Security.

No wonder. This year's modest excess of Social Security tax revenues over outlays is $22 billion and that reduces our unified budget deficit, which is, of course, what needs to be financed each year. I'm wondering if you would be interested in what the official numbers suggest the deficit will be twenty-five years from today? $450 billion annually. Now, imagine the financial markets coming to grips with that one.

And then the argument shifts by the status quo protectors on this so-called "surplus." They say, "Well, the Social Security system," as one person put it to me, "is rather like a pension system, and we should take the longer view"—by which they mean an actuarial view.

I find this a bit odd. The Social Security system today has over $7 trillion of unfunded liabilities. That's just for the retirement system. That's the amount by which all benefits that have been promised to today's participants exceed the scheduled payroll taxes—plus the assets in the trust fund. Incidentally, I collect oxymorons, and I think the Social Security Trust Fund qualifies pretty highly on that score.

A corporate treasurer who would declare a system with $7 trillion of unfunded liabilities in surplus would be committing a career-ending felony in the corporate world.

The total unfunded liabilities, if you put in the health care system and the federal pension system, is $14 trillion, or three-and-a-half times the total debt of America.

Speaking of federal pensions, let me give you another example of unlimited hypocrisy and chutzpa that comes out of Washington. Many of you in business will remember that Congress recently cried with alarm over the fact that the unfunded liabilities for private sector pensions—all of them—rose a stunning $9 billion to $58 billion. They proposed all kinds of faster funding of those pensions. What they did not tell you was that the unfunded pensions, which is the most lavish by far in America for many fewer employees, those in the federal pension system, was $1.1 trillion . . . 25 times the unfunded pensions of all of the private sector workers in America.

Now, if they were not hypocritical, and they were to say, "Why don't we fund the federal pensions on the books the way we require Ford and General Motors and Chrysler and everybody else to do under ERISA [Employee Retirement Income Security Act] requirements over thirty years, that would add almost $100 billion a year, roughly, to the annual budget." That is off the books that no one knows about.

The payroll taxes of our children for Social Security and Medicare are now estimated to go somewhere between 38 and 52 percent of pay. Does anybody think that our kids could pay this much, will pay this much, should pay this much? And the answer on all of these questions, it seems to me, is an unambiguous "no."

Now, who's getting all this largesse? When Franklin Delano

Roosevelt launched the Economic Security Act—and I read it as part of my book project—it's fascinating to see how the world has changed. He saw Social Security in these programs, as he put it, "to prevent destitution," to provide a true safety net from people falling into the basement of the economy.

What's happened to these programs in the last fifty years is quite extraordinary. Both parties—and I try to be bi-partisan in these comments—are very good at scapegoating. Ronald Reagan, for a while, seemed to suggest that the problem of all this spending was the unworthy poor. And that if somehow we could just get those mink-wearing, vodka-drinking . . . Cadillac-driving, welfare queens to stop doing that, we'd solve our budget problems.

Bill Clinton takes the other approach. He argues that if we could just cut the spendings to the fat cats, that would take care of the problem.

The problem is, neither party remembers the Willie Sutton factor, which you know. When asked, "Why did he rob banks?" he said, "That's where the money is."

The money in America now goes largely to people in the broad middle class. And as part of the research on my book, I took all of the federal benefit programs, ran them through the IRS computers, all the tax expenditures, and I found that today about $375 billion a year goes to people above the median income.

Now, some people say you can't change these programs because they're a "contract." That's another of the famous myths, that this is a contract that apparently only goes in one direction. I recall when I was in college taking a course in commercial law. A contract required a meeting of the minds, it was said.

I had a new grandson the other day, and I was in a debate with one of the AARP people arguing this "contract" theory and I said, "My grandson, Peter Carey, is apparently a party to this contract you're talking about. I don't recall that anybody has talked to him about the payroll taxes that he's going to be expected to pay." Also, the Supreme Court has ruled that these are not contracts; logic rules that these are not contracts; what the Congress giveth it can take away.

Now if all of us are on the wagon, which is what's going on now, somebody has to confront a fundamental question, who's going to pull it? Under my proposals for entitlement reforms, I think an important place to start is to face certain unsustainable and inescapable fundamentals that we can no longer ignore.

Before long we will be living six years longer at age 65 than we did, thank God, when these programs were set up. It's perfectly obvious to me that we should increase the retirement age of these programs. And do it gradually to give people a chance to plan for the change—to either age 68 or 70.

We should certainly treat all retirement incomes alike, the way the rest of the world does. You may be shocked to hear the following, in terms of fairness to our children. The median income in America today is something over $30,000–$33,000. I had some experts compute what the tax bill was for a young working family earning median income versus a retired family earning the same amount.

What I discovered was that a typical young working family pays $7,200 in taxes; the retired family pays $900 in taxes. So, the young workers are paying about eight times as much at equivalent incomes as retired elderly.

Finally, we devised something called "the affluence test." The idea is relatively simple. By way of background, every time anybody has tried to reform these programs, the liberals in this world will say, "Well, there those fatcat Republicans go again—they're demolishing the poor." So, I decided it made sense not to create something called "a means test." So, I call it "an affluence test." And I take the position that if those of us who are lucky enough to be above the average income are not willing to cut their benefits, there is no solution to this problem.

So, above the median income I would, on a progressive basis, reduce the benefits so that somebody that's just above the median income loses, let's say, gives up 4 percent of their benefits; and the Pete Petersons of this world lose 75–80 percent of their benefits.

This kind of program would save us $100 billion a year soon. But, because it would go with the demographics, it would be saving us three or four hundred billion dollars a year, not too late in the century.

The other thing I would do, since I guess I'm in the business of offending everyone with this program, is, I would include *all* entitlements.

I was on *60 Minutes* last year [1993] and Leslie Stahl said to me: "You can be on the program as long as you confront the elderly."

So, I put on a metal shield and go out to this retirement community. I show the elderly pictures of my grandchildren. Then I give them some of these numbers. And I said to them, "I'm not a granny basher. I think we're all in this together. You and I are old enough to have been in World War II and we understand the feeling when we think the burden is being shared properly for a worthy goal."

So, I think farmers' benefits, veterans' benefits—for those that are not disabled—and, most certainly, Congressional and federal pensions, should be included so that all of the federal beneficiaries are together and nobody feels that they are being singled out. I happen to think that is a vitally important part of this solution.

Now, let me go to another major driving element of our entitlements—the metastases in health care. I would applaud the President and his wife for putting health care on the top of the agenda. However, I would quickly add, "may his health plan rest permanently in peace."

Something funny happened on the way to the bank. The President appropriately indicated that getting health care costs under control was a principal objective. When I looked at his program originally—and I'm one of the few people that read the 1,342 pages—I was astonished at all of the new entitlements that were being added. Presumably all of these were going to be paid for by a cigarette tax.

So, I called my friend, Warren Rudman, who has a delicious sense of humor. I said, "Rudman, I don't understand how this is going to happen." He said, "Peterson, I thought you were smarter than that. What you do is require everybody to smoke." He said, "That way the revenues are much higher, and people won't be around to collect the early retirement health provisions."

The next solution in this plan, which the Treasury desperately put in when they got into the game far too late, was, they said, "We're going to put caps on these programs, that is, after the fact." Now, if these caps were to have worked, we are to have believed that this Congress, that couldn't get rid of honey bee subsidies, was then going to go back and cut back a whole series of valuable health care benefits, after the fact. In other words, these caps would be made out of rubber and not iron.

Many of you are in business in this audience, so I ask you to just look at your own experience. How easy was it with your own employees the last time that you started to take away a benefit once you had given it to them? Now, if you have trouble doing that, imagine the kind of fun our politicians would have doing that.

The next thing they and Mr. Magaziner tell us is, "Well, our computer models predict the costs accurately." I can say to you,

having looked at all the past estimates of the health care entitlement projections, that they are nothing but what they call in the
computer world "gigo." That's "garbage in, garbage out." Their
numbers always underestimate the costs enormously, and greatly
overestimate the savings. Why? Because there's an iron law of
entitlements: new benefits always create new and much unantici-
pated demand. If, for example, you offer someone long-term
care at home, families are going to provide less of it on their own.
If you offer to subsidize health insurance for early retirees, then
more people are going to quit their work in the 50's and on and
on and on.

As I said, I've looked at all of the projections of costs and then
gone back and said, "What were the real costs?" For the Medicare
system as a whole for the year 1990, we only underestimated the
cost by seven-and-a-half times. That is, they were seven-and-
a-half times larger than the official estimate. It makes no difference whether you're talking about cost estimates for Medicaid,
nursing homes, renal disease, whatever it is, we missed them by
a mile.

The same is true on cost savings estimates. They are always
wildly overestimated. And let me emphasize in a bipartisan way
that the Republican estimates are as egregious as the Democratic
estimates. For example, if you look at the Reagan and Bush estimates of the cost savings, they are as egregious as were the Democratic estimates of cost savings. In other words, in the always
immortal words of Casey Stengel, when it comes to health care
estimates: "We have made too many wrong mistakes."

Now what does all this mean in an approach to health care
entitlement programs? In the first place, I suggest to you, since
we already have an unsustainable program on the books, we must
be very careful about adding new unsustainable programs on
top of old unsustainable programs. It's what they call double jeopardy.

Second, let's approach this problem with something rare in
Washington—profound humility. The melancholy fact is that
when it comes to health care costs, we are all ignorant. None of us
know very much. I believe we should experiment and demonstrate savings before we go on adding a lot of expensive and
expansive new benefits.

Third, I suggest we squarely face root causes of why this
country spends so much more on health care than any other
country. And confront the basic fact that we're going to have to

give up something, if we're going to get this fiscal cancer under control.

And you know what the root causes are as well as I do. First, every health care economist I have read says we have what they call a cost-blind system. Consumers are simply not cost-conscious in America for a whole bunch of obvious reasons.

Secondly, we consume far more high-cost, high-tech and, in many cases, low-benefit health care than any country in the world by far. Just one example. We have eight times more MRI [Magnetic Resonance Imaging] units in America than the Canadians do. Indeed, we have more MRI units in Atlanta than all of Canada.

In this same vein, we spend far more at both ends of life. My second son just had a baby. When I was in the maternity ward, I asked if I could look at the ward for premature babies—the prenatal section. I was astonished to find an area in New York as large as the normal maternity section, filled with crack babies, devices, nurses, specialists, and so forth.

Other countries ask the tough questions. Does it make sense to spend $100,000 a year at the prenatal end for a child that is probably going to have all kinds of problems later? Or would it be better to spend that money elsewhere? The rest of the world answers and asks that tough question—we don't.

At the other end of life, we spend far, far more than any country in the world in the last few months of life. If you don't believe that, go to an intensive care unit in Europe and go to one here. Typically here we've got four to five times as many hospital beds in intensive care. And a large percentage of them are geriatric.

My doctor, the brilliant head of neurology at New York Hospital-Cornell Medical Center Fred Plum says: "We have to strengthen the concept of futility."

He points out—and he's a leading stroke expert that took care of both President Nixon and Jacqueline Onassis—that the truth of the matter is that there are all kinds of diseases for which we can do very little. "In the state of New York," he says, "if you can't demonstrate that the patient is going to die in 48 hours, you are at great jeopardy if you do not use every heroic treatment around."

It's an immensely tough moral, philosophical, political, as well as fiscal issue, that we don't want to talk about.

All of this, of course, is related to very costly defensive medicine. I'm talking about malpractice reform. I'm talking about liv-

ing wills that Richard Nixon and Jackie Onassis and the President
and Hillary have signed. I personally would be open to all kinds
of procedures and incentives to try to encourage more of us to
have them.

Only nine percent of Americans have living wills. Eighty-nine
percent, when they were presented with the concept, said, "I
think it's a good idea." But, they just haven't done it.

So, what I would do on this is to have a minimum no-frills
package. I would put every cost system disincentive that anybody's
heard of. More contributions, more deductibles, more copay-
ments, cap the corporate health care tax breaks exclusion, malpractice reform, encourage living wills. Then, I would admit that
none of us know how much money that's going to save. And only
when we had better knowledge of what all this does to health care
costs and demand would I be talking about some of these expansive new benefits that they are talking about.

This brings me to the final imperative—the political imperative. I've had now over ten years of experience since founding
with five Treasury secretaries something called the Bi-partisan
Budget Appeal. This was a group of 400 CEOs, university presidents, the legal establishment, and so forth. And we were all
trying to promote the idea of cutting spending and getting this
fiscal cancer under control.

And, after the October crash in 1987, we went to the Budget
Summit, trying to get them to face the music. They were seriously
considering our proposal—because we had Democrats and Republicans—when Claude Pepper sent in a video cassette . . .
Claude representing the elderly, AARP, and so forth. And
Claude apparently said in this video: "We're going to demand a
roll call vote, and anybody that is for touching the entitlements,
we're going to get you next November." The Summit meeting just
broke up.

It was then that I realized that a presidential candidate was
right when he told me: "Pete, there is no constituency for fiscal
responsibility. There are constituencies for spending." The
AARP—you can imagine I'm kind of high on their hit list—has
thirty-three million members in America, more than all the citizens of Canada. They've rarely met a new spending program—as
they did recently on health care—they didn't like. They've almost
never met a benefit reduction that they liked. But they dominate
the political scene.

And this is why Warren Rudman, Paul Tsongas and I set up

The Concord Coalition. We have 300 chapters, we have several hundred thousand members. But we know we have to build a grassroots constituency for fiscal responsibility.

Many of you in this audience have children and grandchildren. I can tell you what I've been telling college commencement classes these days. I said, "You young people whose future it is, remind me of the kid in the philosophy class. The old joke in which the philosophy professor says, 'Which is worse, ignorance or apathy?' And some sleepy kid from the audience says, 'I don't know and I don't care.'"

I urged them to have two careers—a career in the private sector and a career as a public citizen. I then urge them to get into a dialogue with their parents, after they've learned the facts, and I said, "Don't you believe that all us middle and old-age fogeys are greedy and avaricious. We may be uninformed. We may be misinformed. We may be ignorant. We may be apathetic. But we love our kids and grandchildren."

But I think if this dialogue does not take place, then we're going to be in important trouble in this country.

So, I end on this note. My parents were Greek immigrants. I learned about the American dream in a very special way. And, while my father would not have put it this way, his role model was the endowment ethic. That is an ethic that cared about what you left to the future. We have now as a country turned to what I call the "entitlement ethic." "I want mine, and I want it here and now." And, fundamentally, it is essential for citizens like you to help our country change from the entitlement ethic to the endowment ethic. Thank you very much.

---

## FACING THE PAINFUL TRUTH: THE 1995 BUDGET DEBATE[5]

It is likely that the second half of 1995 will be consumed by the politics of the national budget. The Republicans have unveiled their proposals to produce a balanced budget by 2002, and

[5]Article by Robert J. Bresler, National Affairs editor of *USA Today*, from *USA Today* 124/2602:15 Jl '95. Copyright © 1995 by The Society for the Advancement of Education. Reprinted with permission.

the Democrats, who have given up on such a goal, are telling the nation how this will be done on the backs of the poor and the elderly.

The facts are well-known. In 1975, the federal debt was 34.5% of the Gross Domestic Product (GDP); today, it has risen to 70% of GDP. Twenty years ago, net interest on the debt was about seven percent of the federal budget; in Fiscal Year 1995, it will exceed 15%. As the size of the budget has grown, so has its composition. In the 1950s, 1960s, and early 1970s, most of the budget was devoted to national defense and discretionary domestic programs. Entitlements were a relatively small portion. For example, the Federal funds devoted to health (largely Medicare and Medicaid) constituted eight percent of the budget in 1975; today, that figure is 18% and threatening to rise dramatically. In 1975, net interest, health expenditures, and Social Security comprised around 34% of the federal budget, as compared to 55% in FY95.

The politics of budget-cutting no longer is a matter of annual appropriations. The discretionary part of the budget that is controlled by the appropriations process has been capped since 1990 at approximately $500,000,000,000. Defense spending has seen a steady decline since 1989. Meanwhile, entitlements (Social Security, Medicare, Medicaid, food stamps, supplemental security income, farm price supports, veterans benefits, federal retirement, unemployment insurance) continue to rise.

Cuts in such programs inevitably bring cries of outrage. In the spring of 1995, the Democrats protested that alterations of the school lunch program was tantamount to taking food from the mouths of babes. Yet, the cuts were minor, only a reduction in the rate of growth, and the program itself comprised a tiny fraction of the federal budget.

Staring the Republican budget-cutters in the face is the simple fact that more than 75% of all the mandatory spending programs are not means-tested. In other words, it is the middle-class, not the poor, who are the major beneficiaries. This is particularly true for Social Security and Medicare—the two largest entitlements.

If Congress ever is to balance the budget, it would have to make substantial changes in entitlement programs. This will involve revising spending formulas and paring benefits. According to the Concord Coalition, a bipartisan group devoted to reducing the deficit, two major changes in the law could lower the deficit by 30%: limiting the cost-of-living adjustment for Social Security to minus two percent below inflation; and lowering benefits from

Social Security and Medicare to families with incomes of $50,000 or more.

These steps are simple only on paper; the politics are horrendous. In a fit of bipartisan irresponsibility, both parties have agreed to take Social Security off the table, at least for now. This apparently irredeemable fact of political life will place a considerable burden on Medicare and the discretionary budget.

Reducing Medicare may be as politically difficult as paring Social Security. The steep cuts in Medicare (perhaps $250,000,000,000 over six years) could involve giving the elderly vouchers to purchase insurance on the private market. This "voucherizing" of Medicare could produce considerable savings by introducing competition into the cost of insurance. On the other hand, such a change would produce a degree of uncertainty into the delivery of health, which could make many older people nervous. It also would incur the wrath of the American Association of Retired People [AARP], one of the most potent and feared lobbies in Washington. The Democratic Party, eager for an issue, would be delighted to take on the mantle as the defender of Medicare. They played that role as the guardian of Social Security in the 1982 elections and deprived Ronald Reagan of his ideological majority in Congress for the remainder of his presidency.

Reducing Medicare is just one step in finding more than one trillion dollars in spending reductions to arrive at a balanced budget by 2002, getting only one-quarter of the way. The discretionary budget will have to face draconian cuts. Invariably, this will require eliminating programs that are the root system of big government. In its proposal for a balanced budget, "Rolling Back Government: A Budget Plan to Rebuild America," the Heritage Foundation suggests privatizing Amtrak, segments of the Postal Service, public housing, and commercial public lands. In addition, it recommends eliminating the Agricultural Extension Service, Soil Conservation Service, Maritime Commission, Bureau of Mines, U.S. Geological Survey, Rural Electrification Administration (now the Rural Utilities Service), and Interstate Commerce Commission (ICC).

The final budget resolution that will emerge from the 104th Congress may not eliminate all of these programs. Nevertheless, if it is going to reach the goal of the balanced budget, any resolution, particularly one that contains tax cuts, will have to propose the elimination of a large number of them.

The ensuing debate will balance the generalized public concern over rising debt against the particularized interest of many constituent groups in maintaining their cherished programs and entitlements. Many will have to see their subsidies, benefit checks, or low-interest loans reduced or eliminated. The rising national debt and the continuous deficit do not constitute an immediate crisis. However, they are depleting national savings, the strength of the currency, and the flexibility of government. If the Republican Party is to claim the moral right to lead this country, they must ask Americans to suffer some deprivations for the sake of the future. The answer can not be postponed much longer.

# IV. FINDING THE WILL

## EDITOR'S INTRODUCTION

The ideological differences between the Republicans and the Democrats were unusually clear during the 1995 effort to balance the budget, an even more divisive process than usual due to the inability of a Democratic President and a Republican-dominated Congress to agree. Section Four is devoted to an examination of the gridlock that has emerged in the recent quest to achieve a 1996 budget. Congress complains of the President's "lack of communication," while the Democrats charge the Republicans with an unwillingness to compromise. As the struggle continues, temporary spending measures approach their deadlines and the nation wonders if another shutdown is imminent.

The first article, reprinted from *U.S. News & World Report*, deals with privatization, in which the government would sell public assets and contract its public services to private corporations, therefore relieving itself of the financial burden while providing the private sector with the benefits of increased work and more income.

The next article in this section "It's Still Feeding Time" is an examination of those discretionary budget programs that resemble but cannot properly be called entitlements. Traditionally they have been called "pork." Maggie Mahar discusses the funding for programs that include defense contracts, nuclear research, space exploration, and shows that cutting the budget should involve more than simply reducing entitlement programs.

Kenneth T. Walsh, in an article called "A Budget Train Wreck" from *U.S. News & World Report*, recognizes that both sides in the budget debate are highly committed to their agendas and their constituencies. Particularly in respect to entitlements, they seem unwilling to back off in order to reach a compromise.

"Guts Check" by Carolyn Lochhead, views the pursuit to balance the budget as a test of power. The Republican Congress's ability to prevail during the current budget and spending debates will determine whether the "GOP dominance is lasting or brief." Because the budget problem is fundamentally political, politicians and lobbyists, with increased determination, will struggle to make their proposals on cutting and spending a reality.

Jim McTague's article "Budget Balancing GOP Senators Get an Edge . . ." from *Barron's* presents the argument among the Republicans in Congress between those who regard tax-cutting as their party's highest priority and those who put balancing the budget above all else.

---

## REVERSING THE TIDE[1]

Representative Scott Klug was nibbling Fritos at his desk in the Longworth House Office Building—another hurried lunch in another frenetic week as House Republicans scramble to transform Washington in a hundred days. A block away, his colleagues were debating $17 billion in recisions from this year's budget, while GOP staffers were looking for additional ways to rein in the cost of government. But Klug, a third-term Republican from Wisconsin, was thinking bigger. As Newt Gingrich's point man on privatization, he wants to wipe out entire lines of government work, from printing to electricity to student loans. "We are bound," declares Klug, "only by our imagination."

A popular concept under Ronald Reagan, privatization is back on the federal agenda at a time when legions of voters think Washington spends too much money and does many things badly. Privatization can take several forms, including selling public assets, contracting services to private vendors and distributing vouchers for the purchase of food or housing from private suppliers. Bill Clinton started the bidding with his 1996 budget, which proposed selling off the government's petroleum reserves and turning air-traffic control over to a government corporation that would raise its own revenue through user fees while operating free of federal budgeting and procurement regulations. Vice President Al Gore, who will unveil round two of his National Performance Review this spring, is studying ways to contract privately for medical research, disaster relief and other services. Ex-

[1]Article by David Hage, Warren Cohen, and Robert F. Black from *U.S. News & World Report* 118/13:42–6 Ap 3 '95. Copyright © 1995 by *U.S. News & World Report*. Reprinted with permission.

plains Elaine Kamarck, one of the centrist "new Democrats" advising Gore: "We are looking at everything and asking: 'Does the government need to be in this business?'"

House Republicans are determined to up the ante. They would cut off federal subsidies to Amtrak, sell the Corporation for Public Broadcasting and privatize the U.S. Postal Service. Clinton would sell four of the government's power-marketing administrations, which supply electricity to several regions of the country, but Klug would sell all five, raising some $11 billion and cutting the federal payroll by 7,300 workers. The Reason Foundation estimates that Congress could raise $77 billion through a one-time sale of government enterprises, saving $12 billion in annual outlays for operating subsidies and interest expense.

**Turning the corner.** Privatization has a long pedigree among free-market analysts. University of Illinois Prof. David Linowes, who headed Reagan's privatization commission, estimates that one fourth of federal workers do jobs that compete with the private sector, such as sweeping floors and repairing trucks. By one estimate, the government could save almost $9 billion a year by giving that work to private contractors, who pay lower wages, employ better technology or take advantage of larger economies of scale. Linowes argues that many government functions, including mail delivery, would be more efficient if driven by the profit motive rather than political dictates. A prime example is Conrail, the nation's Northeast freight railroad, which turned the corner after the government sold it.

Actually, the federal government has a long history of private contracting, not all of it successful. Some 37 percent of spending authorized by Congress each year already goes to private businesses for missiles, medicine, highway construction and other products, according to Donald Kettl, a budget expert at the University of Wisconsin. But contracting has had its share of boondoggles. One vendor in the Superfund environmental cleanup operation, for example, billed Washington for $2.3 million in illegitimate expenses, including tickets to sporting events. And a contractor who promised to save the Army $13.9 million on food service, laundry and transportation at a military base ended up costing taxpayers $600,000 more than if the Army had done the work in-house.

The challenge, say experts such as Linowes and Kettl, is to identify where the private sector offers competition and how Washington can measure its vendors' performance. "The point is not public versus private," asserts Kettl. "It's competition versus monopoly."

**Markets at work.** Few federal programs stand to gain more from privatization than low-income housing. Although 1.3 million families live in public housing, an additional one million remain on waiting lists because of funding shortages. And housing projects in Chicago, St. Louis and other cities have become examples of urban blight.

Last month [March, 1995], the Congressional Budget Office [CBO] estimated that taxpayers could save $1 billion over the next five years by simply halting construction of new public housing and giving tenants vouchers to subsidize their rent wherever they pleased. A voucher system wouldn't completely privatize the system, because local housing authorities would continue to operate some 13,000 projects built and owned by taxpayers. But it would free tenants to shop in the private sector, where contractors can build new housing for as much as 40 percent less than the federal government. That's because private contractors have lower labor costs and less red tape.

Vouchers would have the additional advantage of liberating tenants from the stigma and decay that now plague some housing projects. "If you live in a project, you are often regarded as a pauper," says Linowes. "But if you rent an apartment using a voucher, nobody but the landlord knows."

The voucher approach, tested for years in pilot programs, is a key component of the Clinton administration's plan to overhaul the Department of Housing and Urban Development. HUD would take some $8 billion of construction and operating subsidies now paid to local housing authorities, combine them into one large grant and pay them as housing "certificates" directly to tenants. Renters would be free to stay in public buildings or move to private housing. If they found private-sector housing that was cheaper than government-subsidized public housing, HUD would give them a rebate for a portion of the savings. Housing authorities, after a phase-in period of two years, would have to compete for tenants. "This is capitalism," asserts HUD's Joseph Shuldiner. "This is the discipline of the marketplace."

For now, HUD would plow any budget savings back into renovation funds for local housing authorities so they can compete with private landlords when the time comes. But Shuldiner estimates that the voucher approach could increase the stock of low-income housing by as much as 300,000 units as public-housing residents moved into the private market, leaving their apartments available for others.

The HUD proposal is not without drawbacks. Cheap private-sector apartments are hard to come by in some cities, so even renters with vouchers could face limited choices. And HUD's plan has drawn fire from congressional Republicans, who say it does too little to slow spending and cut red tape. Even so, it is likely to serve as a foundation for the housing policy that emerges from Congress later this year. Rep. Rick Lazio, the New York Republican who chairs the House Subcommittee on Housing and Community Opportunity, is lukewarm to the HUD overhaul, but he says that vouchers "will be used as the basis for restructuring our nation's public housing."

**National treasures.** Market forces that work powerfully in housing may not work as well in the wilderness. Or so Roger Kennedy assumed when he presented the National Park Service's 1996 budget to Congress last month. Much to his surprise, the park service director was asked by committee Republicans to produce a price list that set a market value on each of the nation's 368 park units. "But how," wonders Kennedy, "do you put a price on the Washington Monument?"

In fact, privatizing national parks doesn't make sense to most economists—and not just because Americans would balk at the idea of putting Old Faithful in private hands. For one thing, taxpayers already get a good deal from having parks in the public domain. Half of the National Park Service's full-time rangers work for less than $22,000 a year, even though most have specialized college degrees and put in long hours. Genial rangers in the familiar park service uniforms "are one of the best bureaucracies around," declares Harvard University political scientist John Donahue, precisely because they view public service as a higher calling. Adds Donahue: "They take a lot of their pay in sunsets."

**Competition.** But more fundamentally, parks don't play to the strengths of the marketplace. The whole point of privatization is to tap competition; selling Yosemite to a commercial concern would merely convert a public monopoly into a private one. The park service certainly has its management failings—whole species have been threatened by park overcrowding, while buildings decay for lack of repair funds. But the market is unlikely to correct those mistakes, argues political scientist William Lowry, author of *The Capacity for Wonder*, a critical study of the park service. "Markets work best when they can attach accurate prices to commodities," explains Lowry. But accurate prices require that commodities have substitutes, so buyers and sellers can compare one with another. "When you talk about the Grand Canyon," says Lowry, "there simply is no substitute."

For an agency with a big public trust, the park service actually has privatized a vast array of services—from lodging to food service to trip outfitting. In fact, private concessionaires collected roughly $650 million in revenues from park patrons last year, while the park service itself collected just $76 million in fees— about 5 percent of its budget. In a nod to fiscal pressures in Washington, Kennedy has asked Congress for the power to raise park entrance fees—some of which haven't gone up since 1916— by $32 million. Kennedy also wants to introduce more competition into the bidding process for park concessions, a step that could raise additional franchise revenues.

Even so, Kennedy insists that Washington must draw a line between what properly belongs in the private sector and what should remain public. "When consumers walk into Yellowstone," he says, "they expect something different from what they get in a theme park." As Congress sifts through the privatization lists of Scott Klug and Al Gore, its biggest task may be to decide where the market can rule—and where it cannot.

---

## IT'S STILL FEEDING TIME[2]

When the Pentagon submitted its budget request for 1996, it asked for $236 billion; the defense appropriations bill that Republican leaders hope to slide through Congress sometime in the next few weeks promises around $243 billion—roughly $7 billion more.

Wait a minute. Aren't the Republicans the ones who are dead-set on slashing the federal budget down to its very bone?

Yes—and no. With one hand House members and senators have been cutting federal spending on Medicare, welfare, Medicaid and student loans, but with the other, they've been adding a

[2]Article by Maggie Mahar from *Barron's* 75/3:25 O 23 '95. Copyright © 1995 by Dow Jones & Company Inc. Reprinted with permission.

few billion here, a billion or two there to the '96 budget, "tending to the symbiotic relationships that the congressmen have with contributors and contractors in their home district or state," explains Kim Wallace, a Washington-based political analyst for Lehman Brothers. "It happens every year," he adds. "The Pentagon asks for a little less, and gets a little more."

And it's not only defense contractors who benefit. "In each of the 13 House appropriations bills there is spending that reasonable people would agree is not necessary to further the public interest," says Wallace. "Many would call it 'pork.'"

Of course, the Republicans didn't invent this sweet meat. In the past, Democrats earned the title "porkmeisters," and with good reason. Now that the Republicans are in power, they're merely following a timeworn, if not time-honored, tradition.

"The purebreds amongst the GOP freshmen might want to do nothing but cut the budget even if it hits too close to home, but the old bulls amongst the Republican congressional hierarchy waited too long for the power of the purse to dispense favors to their key money and home-state supporters," explains Ethan Siegal, who heads the Washington Exchange, a Bethesda, Md.-based outfit that analyzes politics and public policy for institutional investors. "And they're doing just that, not only in the appropriations bills, but in the tax bill, which is loaded with special-interest rewards."

What makes such congressional largess raise eyebrows this time around is that it comes amidst a frenzy of budget-cutting. The Republicans had promised to be agents of radical reform. Instead, many of the very same politicians who have been most adamant about slicing the fat out of the roast are, in fact, inserting their own lard.

For investors, this is "a good news/bad news story," writes Siegal in the latest copy of his newsletter. "Those looking for the corporate 'winners' in the Republican budget will find investment opportunities, while those purists who want to see real government reform and a rebirth of the free market with as little government interference as possible will be concerned."

In fact, "many investors do focus on the big picture and worry about the future impact of excessive government spending—and its effect on the credit markets," Siegal added in a recent conversation with *Barron's*. "They would gladly give up the short-term investment opportunity for the greater goal of lower deficits and lower interest rates."

With both points of view in mind, Siegal and his researchers recently took a close look at both the tax bill, which has not yet gone to conference, and the 13 appropriations bills, 10 of them still in what he calls the "sausage-making stage."

Siegal begins by focusing on federal spending that is funneled directly to the private sector. Near the top of the list: "$3.4 billion earmarked for the Department of Energy's solar and nuclear research and development programs, which falls, as usual, into the godfather-like embrace of Senate Budget Committee Chairman Pete Domenici of New Mexico. New Mexico is home to the Los Alamos and Sandia national laboratories, big recipients of DOE funds, so the bulk of that $3.4 billion will almost certainly remain in the budget, deficit or no deficit."

## New Mexicans Shrug at Tax Cutting

Indeed, Domenici turned down a coveted seat on the Senate Finance Committee in order to protect the labs—and the publicly traded companies that have contracts with them. ". . . Senate majority leader Dole asked Domenici to move from the Senate Appropriations Committee to the Finance Committee so that Phil Gramm, Dole's fiercest Senate rival for the Republican Presidential nomination, wouldn't wind up on Finance," explains a former Budget Committee staff member. "Domenici said no—not even as a favor—because while finance is responsible for taxes, the tax code isn't that important to New Mexico. The way Domenici runs money through his state is by staying on the Appropriations Committee, so that he can be on its Energy and Water-Development Subcommittee."

The Commodity Credit Corp. ranks even higher than DOE on the direct-spending list, receiving $7.9 billion to support crop prices, and its money is nearly as safe.

"When the Republicans assumed power, they talked big about cutting big agricultural subsidies," Siegal recalls. "The jury is still out on just how much will be sliced from these programs, but the bottom line is 'not much.' Farm and commodity-state Republicans, led by Sen. Thad Cochran of Mississippi, chairman of the Senate Appropriations Subcommittee on Agriculture, have so far done a pretty good job in thwarting agricultural program reformers." A better job, it seems, than legislators trying to protect the National Institutes of Health's $3.7 billion applied and clinical research program. It too appears among the top five on the direct-spending list and, while it receives less funding, "NIH is slated to take a bigger hit" than the Commodities Credit Corp., notes Siegal.

But isn't the spending justified—don't small farmers need price supports for commodities? Stephen Moore, director of fiscal policy at the Washington-based Cato Institute, dispels any romantic images that urbanites might have of small, family-run sugar plantations: "The truth is that of the 400 classified farm commodities, about two dozen receive more than 90% of the assistance funds, and over 80% of the subsidies enrich farmers with a net worth of more than half a million dollars. Most are businesses with assets in the tens of millions."

The Cato Institute is a libertarian think tank, and Moore believes in letting market forces choose winners; he warns that agricultural subsidies create an uneven playing field: "You're beginning to hear small farmers say that they could compete better in a freer market." As for why smaller farms don't reap a larger share of government help, Moore is matter-of-fact: "Presumably they're not as well-connected politically."

### Party Turncoats Bring Defeat

But agribusiness is. "When Pat Roberts of Kansas, the Republican chairman of the House Agriculture Committee, proposed tough cuts that would have reduced subsidies by some $13.4 billion, Republicans on his own committee voted against him," recalls Wallace of Lehman Brothers. "Four Republicans joined the Democrats—many of the Democrats just wanted to oppose any bill that Roberts sponsored—and Roberts's proposal was defeated. Larry Combest of Texas was flatout saying he just didn't like the way the bill treated farming." As a result, the House Agriculture Committee failed to approve its part of the budget-reconciliation bill.

"The committee abdicated its responsibilities, and the legislation is now in the hands of the House Budget Committee," Wallace explains. "They'll come up with that $13.4 billion somehow—but there's a concern that they won't do it with the care or knowledge that the Agriculture Committee possessed."

Moore views subsidies for agribusiness as just one instance of "corporate welfare." As an easy example he points to the Department of Agriculture Market Promotion Program. It spends $90 million underwriting the cost of advertising U.S. products abroad, with Pillsbury receiving $2.9 million to help peddle muffins and pies, American Legend Mink taking $1.2 million to boost its international sales and McDonald's $465,000 to help introduce the world to Chicken McNuggets.

It's hard to believe, but legislators chose to increase the program's budget by 20% in '96, bringing it up to $110 million. "This decision marks a moment of particular embarrassment for the Republicans," Moore observes, "because the marketing program has become the poster child for pork."

To be fair, Siegal notes that this year the Market Promotion Program was extended with caveats that direct grants not be given to large corporations—but not before California Republican Rep. Frank Riggs tried to exempt wine companies, like those in his home district (Gallo, Sutter Home) from the large-company prohibition. Siegal, a long-time Washington observer, assumes that by next year, "everyone will have figured out a way around the prohibition."

On the tax side, Moore points out more special breaks for corporate farmers, notably $500 million worth of "tax subsidies" for the production of ethanol, a corn-based gasoline substitute. (Ethanol actually enjoys two breaks: a tax credit for companies that blend ethanol and an exemption from federal excise taxes.) This year [1995] there was brave talk of reducing the special treatment. But "the hit on ethanol died a quick death," Siegal writes, as farm-state lawmakers Reps. Jon Christensen of Nebraska and Jim Nussle of Iowa, along with Sens. Cochran of Mississippi, Gramm of Texas and Dole of Kansas—all Republicans—"put the kibosh on the idea."

Archer-Daniels-Midland, the $10 billion agribusiness currently accused of price-fixing, is a major beneficiary of the targeted tax break: "ADM produces 70% of the ethanol used in the United States, and 25% of its revenues are of ethanol and corn sweetener, another heavily subsidized farm product," Moore observes. Coincidentally or not, "ADM and its CEO Dwayne Andreas also have been among the nation's most generous campaign contributors," he adds, "with more than $150,000 in lifetime contributions to Sen. Dole alone."

*Convenient Way To Say Thank You*

But some of the biggest political plums are to be found in the defense appropriations bill. The Cold War may be over, but like the Democrats before them, Republican congressmen often view defense spending as a convenient way to repay generous campaign contributors while simultaneously saving jobs at home.

The Cato Institute's Moore asserts that this means "keeping defense systems and programs of marginal value. They're preserved for domestic reasons, not national-security reasons," he declares. He underlines the perversity of building weapons to keep an assembly line going: "The reason we spend on defense is not to create jobs in a particular district."

Indeed, critics like Siegal contend that if government wants to battle unemployment, there are cheaper and more efficient ways to do it than spending millions to keep workers in jobs where they're manufacturing equipment that's on its way to obsolescence. The problem, as he sees it, is that political pressures override economic considerations when the spending decisions are made: "Rather than making investments in human capital with an eye to long-term economic growth, the decision to create jobs is based on the short-term political needs of a particular legislator representing a particular district."

The defense appropriations bill is still open to several layers of negotiation, but Siegal offers a list of questionable expenditures that he considers most likely to survive. Each is a congressional addition to the Pentagon's original wish list.

Congress plans to provide $2.4 billion of extra funding for two new Marine troop- and equipment-carrying ships, for instance. The larger will cost $1.3 billion and is slated to be built in Mississippi by Litton's Ingalls Shipbuilding. According to both Siegal and Wallace, the appropriation received strong backing from two well-placed Republican senators from Mississippi: Cochran, a member of the Defense Appropriations Subcommittee, and majority whip Trent Lott, a member of the Armed Services Committee. "The smaller ship will cost $974 million and that contract hasn't been awarded yet, but the ship was pushed by both the House and Avondale Industries, which is located in Bob Livingston's home district in Louisiana," Siegal observes. Livingston is chairman of the House Appropriations Committee.

Westinghouse Electric and Rolls-Royce will be the winners if an additional $15.5 million for an ICR Gas Turbine Engine program survives negotiations, and Pennsylvania's Arlen Specter, a member of the Senate Appropriations Committee, is giving the project "heavy backing," according to Siegal's research. The Navy warship engine, a joint project between Westinghouse and Rolls-Royce, would be assembled at the Philadelphia naval yard.

Then there's the $493 billion that Congress is providing for additional B-2 bombers. "Northrop Grumman is the prime contractor on the plane," Siegal reports, "and the $165,000 in campaign contributions that it donated to the GOP members of Congress in just the first six months of this year may have given the effort an extra boost."

Other aircraft that the Pentagon never asked for include six F-15E fighters, costing $311 million, to be built by McDonnell Douglas in Missouri. That's the home state of Republican Christopher Bond, a member of the Senate Appropriations Committee. Also unrequested but in the bill anyway are six F-16C/D jet fighters for an extra $159 million, to be built by General Dynamics in Texas. The Lone Star State is, of course, home to Phil Gramm, contender for the GOP Presidential nomination and member of the Senate Appropriations Committee, and to Republican Henry Bonilla, a member of the appropriations panel in the House. Gramm and Bonilla also helped win $140 million for another OH-58D Kiowa Warrior helicopter built by Bell Helicopter of Texas, a subsidiary of Textron. "The Pentagon had requested just enough funding to upgrade the Kiowa while waiting for the Sikorsky RAH-66 Comanche to come on board," Siegal explains.

Unlike Moore and Siegal, Chuck Gabriel, a defense analyst at Prudential Securities, views additional defense orders purely as investment opportunities, and he offers an even longer list of likely winners. As for concerns about congressional extravagance at a time when the federal debt looms large, he argues that the Pentagon had planned to make most of these funding requests sometime in the next six years anyway; "the appropriations were just moved up to '96."

### Spending Money on Outdated Systems

Siegal disagrees: "It's questionable that these are appropriations that would have been made in the future. First, the defense budget is supposed to go down as a percentage of GDP over the coming years, and secondly, we can't guess which particular weapons we will want to continue to build—no one has yet decided our post-Cold War strategy. The extra spending represents an attempt to lock in as much funding as possible—even though in many cases legislators are spending money to build old weapons systems."

In the coming year, however, Siegal believes that Republicans may regret their largess as they try to explain to voters why they had to pare Medicare and enlarge defense spending. "As voters sense that Republicans are basically no different from Democrats when it comes to coziness between federal dollars and campaign dollars, I think corporate welfare will become a big issue in this election," Siegal predicts. "The Republicans are doing nothing about it—in fact, they're flaunting it. This won't necessarily help Clinton, but it could benefit a third-party candidate trying to tap into the 1992 Perot vote. Perot took 19%, and if those voters are getting all riled up again, it's not so much because of the deficit as because they're fed up with the influence-peddling in Washington."

Siegal could well be right: The Republicans set a higher standard for themselves, and voters may well punish them with that special fury reserved for leaders who make their followers truly believe that change is possible—and then betray that hope.

---

## A BUDGET TRAIN WRECK?[3]

---

At 9:30 a.m. on August 11, [1995] President Clinton sat at a big mahogany table in the Cabinet Room, poured himself a cup of hot tea and convened the first meeting of his "end-game team." For the next hour, a dozen policy makers plotted White House strategy for the inevitable collision with Congress over the budget this fall. Economics adviser Laura D'Andrea Tyson warned that, by mid-October, gridlock could paralyze decision making on the future of Medicare, Medicaid, welfare reform, tax cuts, environmental protection and crime-fighting programs. Budget Director Alice Rivlin said she was making contingency plans to lay off thousands of federal workers because Congress had shown little determination to pass mandatory spending bills by September 30, the end of the fiscal year. And the president acknowledged that

[3]Article by Kenneth T. Walsh and Steven V. Roberts from *U.S. News & World Report* 119/9:36–8 Ag 28 '95. Copyright © 1995 by *U.S. News & World Report*. Reprinted with permission.

such job disruptions could be only the beginning of a string of crises lasting until Christmas.

Washington has had political train wrecks before, but this year's could be the worst yet. Ideological divisions are deeper than ever, the issues are far reaching and a presidential campaign is just beginning, which will further contaminate the rancid atmosphere. One participant at the White House meeting declared that the fall's debates will be "as profound and important" as any since 1964 and 1965, when Congress passed the legislation creating Lyndon Johnson's Great Society.

**Taking on Medicare.** So far, no one is backing off. In mid-August, Democrats and Republicans began attacking each other over Medicare, the health program serving thirty-seven million elderly and disabled Americans that has grown to gargantuan proportions and is central to the budget debate. The Democratic National Committee began an $850,000 television advertising campaign in thirteen states charging that the GOP wants to gut Medicare and undermine the well-being of senior citizens. The Republicans ran commercials in 11 congressional districts charging that selected Democratic House members, including party leaders Richard Gephardt of Missouri and David Bonior of Michigan, are willing to let Medicare go bankrupt by refusing to pare the program to a realistic size.

The public is sending mixed messages. Democratic polls show that 62 percent of Americans oppose deep cuts in Medicare to balance the budget, while GOP polls show that most Americans believe Medicare needs to be reformed or it will go broke. As part of their budget plan, congressional Republicans want to cut the growth of Medicare by $270 billion in order to balance the budget by 2002. They say such cuts are needed to save the system. Clinton, arguing that the GOP cuts are unnecessary and cruel, favors savings of $124 billion as part of his plan to balance the budget by 2005.

Not surprisingly, special interests are gearing up for what could be one of the most extensive lobbying and public-relations efforts in history—on virtually every major issue. "Everybody's got a stake in the debate," says a senior White House official. "The debate will reach everyone the government reaches."

The American Association of Retired Persons, one of the capital's most effective lobbying groups, is mobilizing its thirty-three million members to fight GOP-sponsored Medicare cuts. AARP argues that out-of-pocket costs for the average Medicare beneficiary would increase by too much—$3,400 over seven years—under Republican proposals. "Ultimately, in a debate like this it's what members of Congress hear from home [that counts]," says AARP spokesman Marty Corry. "Medicare, like Social Security, is all about financial security and retirement. It's all about maintaining independence, so you're not a burden on your kids and grandkids."

Meanwhile, the Business Roundtable, a group of two hundred chief executives of major corporations, has allied itself with Ross Perot's United We Stand and other groups in a $10 million advertising campaign to support a balanced budget—without taking a position on the details. "We want to say [to members of Congress] there is a whole group of people out there who simply want you to do it—and you're going to have to do it this year," says Business Roundtable spokeswoman Johanna Schneider. "Without that pressure there is a possibility today that there will not be an agreement."

Despite the president's promise to find "common ground" with his adversaries, the White House has developed a plan to stay on the offensive. Democrats will attack the GOP on at least five fronts when the president returns from his vacation in Wyoming and Hawaii in September: Medicare, education, the environment, teen smoking and assault weapons. First, the White House will continue to accuse Republicans of slashing Medicare too deeply as they cut taxes for the rich. Then administration officials will blast the GOP for cutting college loans, "gutting" environmental programs, siding with the tobacco industry in the fight against teen smoking and allying itself with the National Rifle Association by supporting repeal of the ban on semiautomatic assault-style weapons. "The Republicans are lining up with the special interests—the chemical companies, the tobacco companies, the NRA, the rich," says a Clinton strategist. "It's an open invitation for us to steal the swing suburban vote."

**Fight for the future.** The Republicans, however, are convinced that the country will reward them for making tough choices on balancing the budget, cutting the growth of social programs, toughening standards for welfare and other issues. "This is not a game," says pollster Frank Luntz, an adviser to House Republicans. "It's a fight for the future of the country. It's a fight to the death."

So far, the Republican-led Congress hasn't broken any records for speedy action. The House has approved 11 of the 13 spending bills needed to keep the government running, but the

Senate has approved only six of them. Senate moderates are balk-
ing at some of the more stringent provisions, such as a 15 percent
spending reduction at the Interior Department, and the president has threatened to use his veto pen. White House aides say he
is most likely to nix three huge spending measures: a bill covering
the Departments of Labor, Health and Human Services, and Education; a measure covering the Departments of Veterans Affairs
and Housing, the Environmental Protection Agency and independent agencies, and a defense bill.

Parts of the government will shut down unless these bills are
enacted by October 1 or unless Congress passes a stopgap spending measure known as a continuing resolution. The differences
are so severe—between Republicans and Democrats, between
Congress and the White House, and among Republicans themselves—that the deadline could easily be missed.

Another potential for gridlock will come when Congress considers legislation allowing the government to exceed its current
$4.9 trillion debt ceiling. Scores of conservative Republicans who
were elected as budget balancers are reluctant to support that
authorization, but White House officials warn that the government could default on some of its obligations if the measure is
delayed too long. The government probably has enough borrowing authority until late October or early November, giving Congress a bit of breathing room.

**Uncertain results.** Adding to the general rancor are deep
divisions over a reconciliation bill designed to keep federal spending on track with overall budget goals. That legislation includes
many controversial issues on which there is no consensus, such as
tax cuts for families and the well-to-do, a reduction in the capital-
gains tax, and possibly Medicare, Medicaid and welfare reform.
There is no way to predict any of the outcomes.

For his part, Clinton will leave the day-to-day bargaining to his
aides. "You'll see the president rise above it all," says a senior
White House official. "That's what the American public wants. He
won't be negotiator in chief." Instead, the president is considering a prime-time address from the Oval Office and a series of
speeches to argue that his administration's budget priorities reflect fundamental values such as creating opportunity and requiring citizens to take responsibility for their own success.

But some White House strategists say Clinton's best option,
considering the hostile atmosphere, might be to postpone major
decisions and negotiate a truce. The goal would be to fully debate

national priorities during the 1996 campaign. By then, however, it may be too late to satisfy the voters. "There is a very strong feeling out in the country," says political scientist Stephen Hess of the Brookings Institution, "that Washington should do something now—or there will be a pox on both houses."

## GUTS CHECK[4]

Fresh from the victories of their first hundred days as Congress's new majority, Republicans stand on the brink of an epic clash over federal spending whose outcome will set the nation's economic course for years to come, and determine whether GOP dominance is lasting or brief.

Republicans are resolved to balance the budget by 2002, the supreme vow that undergirds their aim to shrink government and restore the nation's fiscal integrity. But like Pickett's troops before their suicidal charge at Gettysburg, they find themselves facing daunting and possibly overwhelming odds. Not since 1931 has the budget been balanced with any consistency. Doing so would change the course of 20th-century government.

At Gettysburg, a handful of the southern troops who charged the Union fusillade survived to reach the enemy line, only to fall at the spot historians now call the high watermark of the Confederacy. Republicans today declare this to be their historic moment, and speak bravely of courage, boldness, and the nation's salvation for unborn generations. Yet still a sense of dread is evident among even the most enthusiastic GOP troops. They know that this summer's struggle could mark the high point of their own war against the immense forces that have spawned the modern state.

Like many Republicans on Capital Hill, Sen. Bill Frist, the Tennessee heart surgeon who came from nowhere to defeat Democrat Jim Sasser last November, said he will fight to the death. "I've been in medicine for the last twenty years," says Frist, sitting in his Capitol Hill office one afternoon in March, "and I'm going to be here for six or twelve years and leave the Senate after

[4]Article by Carolyn Lochhead from *Reason* 27/3:20–5 Jl '95. Copyright © 1995 by *Reason*. Reprinted with permission.

that. I have a finite time in which to accomplish my mission . . . and suffer whatever ramifications there are from a political standpoint."

Republicans know that they must scale back or end scores of programs that are just as popular with their own allies as with their foes. Business subsidies have to be slashed along with Democratic favorites like welfare and public television. And as a cold matter of arithmetic, Republicans must take on the huge middle-class welfare programs called entitlements.

They also know that to mess with middle-class welfare is to violate the first principle of American political survival. The last time they tried it, in 1986, it cost them the Senate.

Entitlements are programs that automatically pay benefits to anyone who asks and qualifies. The scariest one for Republicans is Medicare, the health care program for the elderly. Second only to Social Security in the pantheon of sacred cows, it is careening wildly out of control, its "trust fund" going into the red next year. Medicare will be the decisive battlefield in this year's budget war.

"The real problem is that the public wants to have its cake and eat it too," says a top Republican Senate aide. "These programs exist for a reason. There are well-organized and identifiable groups that benefit. A lot of people are getting more than they're putting in, and the elderly especially are getting a nice deal."

The political landscape right now, he says, "is very uncertain. Nobody knows where it's going."

Half of all Americans now receive some form of entitlement, whether Social Security, Medicare, Medicaid, Aid to Families with Dependent Children, unemployment insurance, veterans benefits, federal pensions, food stamps, school lunches, the earned-income tax credit, farm subsidies, or disability payments.

Entitlements consume more than half of the $1.5-trillion budget. They are driving the chronic $200-billion deficits, which will double to $421 billion by 2005. The General Accounting Office, the Congressional Budget Office, the Office of Management and Budget, and the Bipartisan Commission on Entitlements and Tax Reform have all charted the budget's calamitous current course and urged quick action.

Interest on the debt, at $203 billion, is now the third-largest item in the budget, consuming nearly as much as all domestic programs combined. Interest payments will overtake the entire defense budget in just five years. By 2012, entitlements and interest on the debt will consume all federal tax revenue, leaving no money for anything else: no Head Start, no national parks, no highways, no courts, no Pentagon.

Already, government borrowing is absorbing fully half of all U.S. savings, draining the economy of investment in the future productive capacity vital to higher living standards. Gargantuan government borrowing is already depressing the economy.

When the baby boom, now in middle age, begins to retire in just fifteen years, entitlement costs will explode and the nation will find itself in financial crisis. Entitlements must be contained, not just to balance the budget, but to prevent a ruinous decline in living standards and a crushing tax burden on future generations.

Republicans, not entirely by design, are making it their crusade to avert this calamity. The keystone pledge of the Contract with America was the constitutional amendment to balance the budget. Republicans hoped it would give them the political cover to begin controlling a Great Society run amok.

But on March 2 [1995], when the amendment fell one vote short in the Senate, the GOP found itself out on a plank that had just been sawed off.

The amendment "would have brought the president to the table," said a rueful Pete Domenici, chairman of the Senate Budget Committee, just before the measure went down. "It would have brought many of the parties that are out there warring over their own money and their own programs to the table, because the will of the sovereign states and the people would say we can't continue what we're doing. That was the strength of it. Without that, it's going to be very, very difficult."

In the fight to pass the amendment, Republicans deeply committed themselves to balancing the budget without it. Any retreat now, they are convinced, would doom them. This is their moment, they contend. "There's a big risk in politics," says Rep. Bill Baker (R-Calif.). "The disaster awaits us if we don't take that risk."

But many fear that taking the plunge could doom them too. John Danforth, the retired Missouri Republican senator who co-chaired the entitlements commission, says tackling entitlements "could be political suicide. That's why they haven't been dealt with in the past."

The budget problem is fundamentally political. The government could continue to grow at 3 percent a year and still get to a balanced budget in seven years, because tax revenue climbs continually as the economy grows. The problem is that many programs are growing much faster than that. Medicare is expanding by more than 10 percent a year; it will cost $174 billion this year and balloon to $272 billion in five years. Along with Medicaid, the health program for the poor, Medicare is the root of the federal deficit and the chief obstacle to balancing the budget.

It also provides health care to thirty-two million elderly at bargain-basement prices. Current retirees are getting about five dollars in benefits for every dollar they paid in payroll taxes, and the deal gets better every year. The Urban Institute's Eugene Steuerle estimates that the lifetime value of Medicare benefits for an average retiring couple will increase an astonishing $100,000 over the current decade: from $186,100 in 1990 to $278,600 by 2000.

The GOP is about to get a dose of bitter medicine, as the same health-industry groups that helped defeat President Clinton's government takeover of health care—a defeat that helped sweep the GOP to a landslide in November [1994]—now wage all-out war to prevent any federal retreat from health care.

The American Association of Retired Persons [AARP] is already gunning for the GOP. Industry groups are preparing versions of "Harry and Louise" ads to attack Medicare and Medicaid changes. Even the GOP governors are working overtime to preserve their Medicaid money. Washington policy analysts are already wondering out loud if health care will turn out to be Bill Clinton's ticket to re-election after all.

"To make this big change in spending and taxing is going to be extremely difficult," says the GOP aide, "and I don't think even the members are all fully aware of how difficult it will be—although they are starting to get an idea—nor is the public aware."

The one big success Democrats scored in the GOP's first hundred days was to stop the Balanced Budget Amendment, and they did it by claiming the measure would "plunder" the Social Security "trust fund," blithely ignoring the fact that the so-called trust fund is being "plundered" now. The argument was completely disingenuous, but it worked.

Rolling back government is much easier in the abstract than in its specifics, not only for politicians, but also for the public. Politicians' hypocrisy often simply mirrors the public's. Republicans rightly decry the willingness of liberals to finance their compassion with other people's money. But conservative voters also prefer to cut other people's programs while saving theirs, like farmers who bank hundreds of thousands of dollars in crop subsidies while denouncing welfare mothers.

Sen. Richard Lugar, a Republican running for president, has demonstrated that political courage does exist, offering a plan to phase out the farm subsidies that go to his own Indiana constituents. But sitting right next to him as he testified to the Senate Budget Committee in February was North Dakota Democrat Kent Conrad, fresh from killing the Balanced Budget Amendment. Conrad had been arguing that Congress can balance the budget without an amendment, but that day he was busy insisting that farm subsidies have to be off the table.

Conrad has a big Republican friend over in the House, where Kansan Pat Roberts has been holding Agriculture Committee field hearings that seem designed to undermine Lugar. The witness lists read like a subsidy pep rally: Mr. Don Crane, Ford County Wheat Growers; Mr. Larry Kepley, Farm Credit System; Mr. Otis Molz, Farmland Industries; Mr. Larry Williams, Kansas Bankers Association; Mr. Rod Lenz, Colorado Potato Administrative Committee; Mr. Dave Carter, Rocky Mountain Farmers Union, and on and on in an endless parade indistinguishable from the ones former Democratic chairman Kika de la Garza used to run.

The spectacle that raged over the $16 billion package of spending cuts in this year's budget, known as rescissions, offered another telling portent. The cuts unleashed howls of protest from Democrats who portrayed each trim as a mean-spirited attack on the poor to pay for tax cuts for the rich. Yet they totalled a mere 1 percent of the $1.5 trillion federal budget.

California Republican Jerry Lewis, chairman of the House Appropriations subcommittee that came up with $9.5 billion of the House package, emerged from the exercise furious at his own colleagues. "There are significant chinks in our armor as we go to battle at serious budget time," Lewis warns. "Unless we are willing to regroup and rethink, then we are absolutely whistling in the proverbial wind."

Lewis points to the $206 million reduction he proposed for the behemoth $38 billion veterans program. Knowing that the notoriously ill-managed veterans hospitals are nonetheless "sensitive and controversial," Lewis says he decided to preserve spending levels at the level requested by President Clinton, plus a

House add on. He said he sought only to eliminate more money that had been added by the Senate for six ambulatory care facilities. President Clinton immediately excoriated this half-a-percent trim that left spending higher than his own request as an ugly assault on veterans.

Then when cutting time arrived, Lewis says, Bob Stump (R-Ariz.), the chairman of the Veterans Affairs Committee, and Gerry Solomon (R-N.Y.), chairman of the Rules Committee, led the retreat, saying they wanted to restore the money before the Democrats did.

"When you got right down to it, they weren't even willing to take that step," Lewis says. "People say, 'Cut spending, but make sure government fills the pothole in front of my house.' When people who are the biggest of budget cutters have programs that they're emotionally involved in—even though they are huge programs—there's not a dime of it that can afford to be considered."

If such timidity, Lewis says, "is a reflection of the real intestinal fortitude" in both parties, "then there are real problems in the House of Representatives before you even get to the Senate."

The Senate, of course, is led by Bob Dole, the new media darling now viewed by liberals as the pillar of moderation who will turn back the House barbarians. In a *New York Times* profile, the Senate Republican leader and number-one contender for the GOP presidential nomination said his message would be, "reining in government and all that other stuff."

Dole often sounds eerily reminiscent of George Bush, resorting to Bushisms when trying to articulate the GOP message of smaller government and other elements of "the vision thing." His lieutenants who chair the big committees—Mark Hatfield, Robert Packwood, Nancy Kassebaum, John Chafee, Larry Pressler, William Roth, and Arlen Specter—are cool if not hostile to a major rollback in the federal government.

But even the staunchest Senate conservatives have tasted the joys of the status quo. "This is going to be very tough politics for these guys for the first time," says a Democratic committee aide. "They've always had it easy going around saying the government's the problem, and yet when it comes down to brass tacks, those guys are parochial politicians just like everybody else up here."

He recalls an episode in the transportation committee when the administration laid out plans to cut Amtrak. Mississippi's Trent Lott, the GOP whip who won the job on the strength of his conservative credentials, "all of a sudden discovered that there was an Amtrak line going from Chicago to New Orleans, and guess where it went through," the aide recalls. "All of a sudden he said, 'Well now, you guys have to work with us. You're springing this on us,' and he was back pedaling like mad. All these years conservatives, including Lott, have been saying, 'Amtrak, that's socialism.' So it's going to be tough going for them."

One little corner to watch this summer, the Democrat suggests, is LIHEAP, the low-income energy assistance program, a relic of Jimmy Carter's disastrous reaction to the "energy crisis" of the 1970s. LIHEAP pays the utility bills of an extravagant number of New Hampshire residents who will vote in the bellwether GOP presidential primary.

"We're going to watch what Mr. Gramm and Mr. Dole and Mr. Specter have to say about LIHEAP," the aide says. He says he knows what New Hampshire Republican Judd Gregg will say, "because we went through this last year," when the administration proposed reducing LIHEAP. "Judd Gregg and Trent Lott said, 'Oh no, no, no, you can't cut LIHEAP.' LIHEAP also goes for air conditioning in Mississippi, and they said, 'Oh, no, no, no, you can't do that. This is an important public program.'"

Rolling his eyes at the mention of LIHEAP, a GOP staffer acknowledges the inconsistency. "The word *courage* is a political cliché," he says, "but courage is really what they need right now."

Even the 73 vaunted GOP House freshmen at the vanguard of the revolution understand the value of pork. The day after the $189 billion tax cut in the Contract with America passed the House, Andrea Seastrand, a grass-roots conservative from California's central coast, faxed dual press releases: "Seastrand Praises Middle Class Tax Relief Bill," and "Niblick Bridge Survives: Seastrand Fights to Keep Money for Paso Robles Bridge Expansion."

That little bridge happens to be the same one that sparked a citizens' rebellion when the Paso Robles city council first proposed paying for it years ago through a colossal tax on local property owners. So the city council turned to Congress, which stuck the tab with federal taxpayers, in Iowa and other far-flung places, who will never cross the Niblick Bridge.

Such are the homely illustrations of the great forces that built the New Deal, the Great Society, and other 20th-century versions of socialist democracy. They will not die easily.

UCLA economist William Allen, now retired, often made the

point that socialism leads to two things: poverty and tyranny. The extent will vary depending upon how far the experiment is tried, he said, but the direction always holds. Yet while the invisible hand of the market produces a better if not perfect outcome, Allen noted that free markets lose in the political arena, precisely because the invisible hand is invisible.

The hand of government by contrast, is nothing if not visible. Its actions are advertised by every politician. Advocating a hands-off policy seems a hard-hearted excuse to do nothing about grievous social problems. That government usually creates further problems while failing to solve the first one matters less than that it tries.

Then there is the modern secular theology of compassion, which trades in Mother Teresa's philosophy for Ted Kennedy's. While the old Catholic nun labors in the slums of Calcutta, the U.S. senator ministers to the poor from the marbled Senate offices of the Russell Building without ever getting his hands dirty.

Senatorial compassion conveys a sense of spiritual well-being not only to those who exercise it, but to those who support it. Government good works offer more than the ostensible aid they lend to the needy; they also allow people to feel good about themselves by voting for the politician who donates tax money to good causes. Like market successes, however, the policy failures that result are often hidden within the larger milieu.

Still, despite such powerful forces, the outlook is hardly all bleak for the GOP agenda. The House's success with the *Contract With America*—a sweeping package of tax cuts, welfare reform, tort reform, regulatory reform, and congressional reform—was without legislative precedent in modern times. Nine out of the ten items passed, defying earlier predictions among even its supporters.

Democrats were routed so thoroughly that 58 percent of them crossed party lines to vote for the very thing they had said they despised.

The shift in the political discourse and terms of debate has been extraordinary. Democrats seem in shock. At a welfare hearing, Democratic Representative Charles Rangel of New York was amazed that GOP witness Lawrence Mead of Princeton University urged recipients to find immediate work, even at the minimum wage.

"If you're a high school dropout, you don't just pick up *The New*

*York Times* and find out what jobs are out there," Rangel remonstrated. "What should [that person] do, just hit the streets?"

"Yes, exactly," Mead responded.

An energetic and unapologetic conservatism has taken over the House, not only opening debate on matters long bottled up by the old leadership, but demonstrating their extraordinary popularity, even among Democrats.

The change could hardly be more profound. Rather than Chicago Democrat Dan Rostenkowski presiding over his Ways and Means Committee fiefdom, there sits Texas conservative Bill Archer, who not only vows to "pull the income tax up by its roots," but has people believing him.

The ideological division has crystallized and sharpened. The debates reflect real struggles over very different visions. "I have a simple message for the Democrats," Archer declared as he opened the tax-cut debate. "It is not your money. It is the taxpayers' money. It does not belong to the government. It belongs to the workers who earned it."

The '60s-style protests against the changes have generated scant interest. Few even noticed when Patricia Ireland, president of the National Organization of Women, got herself arrested in the Capitol Rotunda during debate on the Republican welfare bill.

Demonstrators bused in by the union-backed Philadelphia Unemployment Project tried to disrupt a welfare hearing but seemed more successful at undermining their supporters. "I do job training," shouted protester Leona Smith. "I teach job training. And there ain't no jobs." They were escorted outside, where they continued their protest on the steps mainly to reporters.

Democrats remain in a highly reactive mode. They protest every cut and defend every program, but suggest no alternative.

They offer only more job training programs that a large body of serious studies shows don't work. They reach for transparent hyperbole, comparing proposals to slow the growth of welfare spending to the Nazi Holocaust. Reductions, they said, will "savage" babies, kids, widows, pregnant women, and the elderly. Are puppies next, one has to wonder? The proposals they do offer often are variations on GOP themes, such as their insistence on workfare.

Florida Democrat Sam Gibbons, a Great Society architect, finally grew apoplectic, screaming on the House floor, "You all sit down and shut up! Sit down and shut up!"

Republicans have a potent budget weapon in hand, if they choose to use it. If the House refuses to fund a program, or cuts its spending, the matter can end there. The so-called zero-out option grows from the simple constitutional fact that both houses of Congress must approve money for the discretionary programs that Congress funds each year.

"It doesn't matter what the other chamber does, and it doesn't matter what the president does," says House Appropriations Committee Chairman Robert Livingston. "You can't veto a zero."

The power is as old as the Constitution, but Democrats spent their forty-year reign in the House creating programs, not killing them. House Republicans now promise to exercise this enormous power of the purse to roll government back.

House Appropriations Chairman Lewis warns of the danger of timidity. If the GOP fails to balance the budget but manages through small cuts to anger a passel of constituencies, he says, "We could be laying the seeds of a political disaster."

California's Chris Cox, a member of the House leadership, is certain that Republicans learned from the Reagan administration's budget battles, which ultimately succeeded in eliminating just four programs and left federal spending higher than ever. "Nobody likes taking all of the heat for cutting food stamps when in fact, they are still increasing," Cox says. "If somebody is going to be criticized for spending less on food stamps, then by God, we ought to spend less on food stamps."

There is, he said, "a political calculus at work. What will dawn on every living soul in the Republican Party is that it makes no sense whatsoever to take heat for cutting spending while failing actually to do it. The irony is that the viciousness of the attacks from the left in the face of modest trimming of spending growth will in the end virtually require trenchant cuts."

The Senate GOP aide believes his party is riding a long-term rightward shift in the country. Ronald Reagan ultimately lost his budget wars, but he was at the leading edge of that shift, this strategist argues. Still, he concedes, much political residue lingers from forty years of Democratic control.

"We are talking about huge changes, and big changes like this just don't happen overnight," he said. "Rome wasn't burned in a day." Republicans may, he says, have to regain the White House and consolidate their hold on Congress before they can fundamentally alter the direction of government.

GOP strategists are urging boldness. In a memorandum, Jeff

Eisenach, a close adviser to House Speaker Newt Gingrich, said the public first must be convinced that change is vital. Eisenach recommended a "burning platform" message, borrowed from the true story of a man on a burning North Sea oil rig. He jumped hundreds of feet into a freezing ocean littered with burning debris because he knew he would die if he didn't.

In his Senate office, Frist turns to a group photograph that hangs on the wall. "These are people I transplanted back two years ago," the former surgeon says. "All these people have heart transplants or lung transplants. That little baby was five days old when I transplanted him. Then some of these people here are as old as 65." He turns back from the photograph and says, "So to give that up, I need to make sure that we accomplish certain things, and if not, I shouldn't be here."

Even Frank Riggs, a political straddler from California's north coast, a district divided between those who want to cut trees and those who want to hug them, voices stoic commitment. Defeated after his first term when Clinton won in 1992, he signed the Contract last September [1994] and regained his seat in November's GOP tide.

"I've gone through what I call a political near-death experience, and it's truly emboldened and liberated me," Riggs says. "There is life after Congress, and politics should never be the be all, end all. And I believe, to my core, what Henry Hyde [the Illinois Republican who chairs the House Judiciary Committee] told me when I first came back here: that in politics, there are things worth losing for."

The most important thing Republican budget cutters have on their side may be the budget's own naked reality. "My hope is that when the American people are faced with the reality of the problem, they're going to decide that this has to be done," says Danforth. "We need to go directly to the public and [discuss] what it is we are doing to our children and our grandchildren and to the future of the country. We are doing something terrible."

Danforth concedes that this argument has not resonated with the public before and that it may not resonate now. "But at least we have to raise the issue," he says. "If the issue is raised clearly to the American people, then in a democracy the people decide. And if the people decide we want ours now, take care of us and forget about our children, then at least that is a conscious decision."

## BUDGET-BALANCING GOP SENATORS GET
## AN EDGE IN BETTING ON WHETHER AND
## WHEN CONGRESS WILL CUT TAXES[5]

The cherry and dogwood trees are in full bloom here, but it is the sweet fragrance of tax reform that hangs thick over Capitol Hill. Gingrich, Armey, Archer, Lugar, Domenici and Nunn, and let us not forget what's-his-name in the White House, all have proposals that promise to lessen the federal tax bite. Will anything come of them in time for the next 1040? For an answer we turned to Rick Grafmeyer, the national director of tax and legislative services for Ernst & Young and a former staff member of the Senate Finance Committee.

"If there's a bill, it will be very modest," he says.

The outcome will be the result of a tug of war under way between Senate Republicans. On one side are the likes of Pete Domenici of New Mexico, who wants to get deficit reduction out of the way before taking on taxes, and on the other are the allies of Phil Gramm of Texas, who wants to cut spending and taxes simultaneously (otherwise, Gramm says, the public might perceive the GOP as breaking its *Contract With America*).

Grafmeyer gives a slight edge to the budget balancers. He expects them to adopt a limited version of the House's Contract With America Tax Relief Act of 1995, which in its unadulterated form has provisions pleasing to most major constituencies. The House bill offers tax breaks for families, for married couples, for senior citizens on Social Security, for people dying of AIDS and other diseases, for big businesses paying the alternative minimum tax, and for small-business owners who want to pass the enterprise on to another family member.

The more radical proposals that set out to scrap the current tax system—things like Rep. Dick Armey's 17% flat tax—won't get serious scrutiny until 1997—assuming a Republican takes the White House—says Grafmeyer. All the talk now is just laying the foundation for the future debate.

"There might be a window of opportunity in 1997 for the new

[5]Article by Jim McTague from *Barron's* 38 My 8 '95. Copyright © 1995 by *Barron's*. Reprinted with permission.

President to make a radical change because there's usually a honeymoon period," he says. The window doesn't guarantee success, however. He reminds his clients that Bill Clinton had the same kind of opportunity to reform the nation's health-care system in 1992 and blew it.

Grafmeyer said there's an impressive drive in the Senate to put balancing the budget above all else. The feat would present Clinton with a dilemma on the eve of the next Presidential election: to veto or not to veto? It would be a no-win situation for the President. If he were to sign a budget-balancing bill, the GOP would be able to boast that it was able to walk a high, thin public-policy wire from which Mr. Clinton plummeted earlier in his term. If he were to veto the bill for whatever reason, be it compassion for welfare recipients or partisan politics, he runs the risk of bringing on himself and his party the blame for all subsequent recessions, stagflations, market meltdowns and other financial ailments.

Budget balancing will require the GOP to expend huge amounts of will power. The growth of welfare and Medicare will have to be slowed considerably, which will generate considerable controversy. Democrats already are warning senior citizens that the GOP will weaken their health safety net to cut the taxes of the very rich. To stay the course, the Senate GOP will need the cooperation of most of its 55 members. Therefore, Grafmeyer predicts, the leadership will try to appease members who are adamant about cutting taxes by giving them a few of the goodies offered in the House bill.

Domenici is already under attack from members of his own party. On April 27, Dan Coats of Indiana and 11 other Republican senators sent him a letter expressing their firm commitment to the $500-per-child tax credit contained in the House bill. "For too long the family has been ignored," the letter said. "Clearly, the Republican budget will be incomplete if the family is not a priority." Co-signers included John Chafee of Rhode Island, John McCain of Arizona, Robert Smith of New Hampshire, Larry Craig of Idaho, Mike DeWine of Ohio, Spencer Abraham of Michigan, Conrad Burns of Montana, Kaye Bailey Hutchison of Texas, Lauch Faircloth of North Carolina, Dirk Kempthorne of Idaho and Rodney Grams of Minnesota. Their budget-balancing colleagues may throw them a bone.

One unknown in this contest of wills is the amount of lobbying pressure that will be brought to bear by the broad coalition of groups that supported the House bill, which included families, seniors, Christian fundamentalists and the U.S. Chamber of Commerce.

The Chamber thinks the Contract's tax provisions with its reduction in capital-gains rates and its tax-free savings accounts is a terrific way to spur savings and investment. "If Congress gets nothing done in the way of an alternative tax system, the House bill is an improvement," says Martin Regalia, the business group's chief economist. "It moves in the right direction." Lawmakers, as we all know, occasionally buckle under to pressure from powerful lobby groups. So it's possible that the Senate could be a more generous tax-cutter than Grafmeyer predicts.

There's also bound to be pressure from the House when the Senate versions of the budget and tax plans go to a conference committee for the two chambers to work out a compromise. Some prominent House members—including Ways and Means Chairman Bill Archer of Texas, a proponent of a consumption-based tax—have begun talking about the Contract's tax provisions as a necessary interim step between the current system and a simplified one. They reason that if the GOP delivers the House package before 1997, it could argue more convincingly during the Presidential campaign that a total overhaul of the unpopular tax system is just a matter of getting their man or woman in the White House.

Without some meaningful tax action this year, the public might quickly become skeptical, especially when it becomes apparent that a total overhaul of the system would have to be gradually phased in for up to ten years after passage to avoid serious economic dislocations.

# BIBLIOGRAPHY

An asterisk (*) preceding a reference indicates that the article or part of it has been reprinted in this book.

### BOOKS AND PAMPHLETS

Bird, Richard M., Ebel, Robert D.; & Wallich, Christine, eds. Decentralization of the socialist state. World Bank. '95.

Brashear, David. Government in crisis. Chesapeake River. '91.

Burdekin, Richard C. K. & Langdana, Farrokh K. Confidence, credibility, and macroeconomic policy. Routledge. '95.

Calleo, David P. The bankrupting of America. Morrow. '92.

Cebula, Richard J. Federal budget deficits. Lexington. '87.

Cogan, John F.; Muris, Timothy J.; & Schick, Allen. The budget puzzle. Stanford University Press. '94.

Dugas, Christine. Fiscal fitness. Andrews & McMeel. '95.

Eichengreen, Barry J., Frieden, Jeffry A.; & Hagen, Jurgen von. Monetary and fiscal policy in an integrated Europe. Springer-Verlag. '95.

Elston, Julie Ann. U. S. tax reform and investment. Avebury. '95.

Frankel, Jeffrey A. Financial markets and monetary policy. MIT Press. '95.

Gold, Steven D., ed. The fiscal crisis of the states. Georgetown University Press. '95.

Gurumurthi, S. Fiscal federalism in India. Vikas. '95.

Heilemann, Ullrich & Reinicke, Wolfgang H. Welcome to hard times. Brookings Institution. '95.

Herman, Edward. The federal budget. Pierian. '91.

Heuser, John. A citizen's guide to the federal budget. R & E. '92.

Hirsch, Werner Zvi & Rufolo, Anthony M. Public finance and expenditure in a federal system. Harcourt. '90.

Ippolito, Dennis S. Uncertain legacies. University Press of Virginia. '90.

Jain, Chaman L. & Tomic, Igor M. Essentials of monetary and fiscal economics. Graceway. '95.

Jones, David M. The buck starts here. Prentice-Hall. '95.

Liner, Charles D., ed. State and local government relations in North Carolina. University of North Carolina. '95.

Lynch, Thomas Dexter. Federal budget and financial management reform. Quorum. '91.

Mayer, Thomas & Sheffrin, Steven M. Fiscal and monetary policy. Elgar. '95.

McNamara, Joseph S. The federal budget. Hillsdale College Press. '87.

Morgan, Iwan W. Deficit government. Dee, I. R. '95.

Sample, V. Alaric. The impact of the federal budget process on national forest planning. Greenwood. '90.

Schick, Allen. The federal budget. Brookings Institution. '95.

Schmidt-Hebbel, Klaus. Colombia's pension reform. World Bank. '95.

Sumberg, Alfred D. Education budget alert for fiscal year 1994. Committee for Education Funding. '93.

Thai, Khi V. Structural budget deficits in the federal government. University Press of America. '87.

Zimmerman, Joseph Francis. State-local relations. Praeger. '95.

ADDITIONAL PERIODICAL ARTICLES WITH ABSTRACTS

For those who wish to read more widely on the subject of the Federal Budget, this section contains abstracts of additional articles that bear on the topic. Readers who require a comprehensive list of materials are advised to consult the *Reader's Guide to Periodical Literature* and other Wilson indexes.

**The Peterson sacrifice test.** Peter G. Peterson. *Across the Board* 31:56–7 F '94

Adapted from Facing Up: How to Rescue the Economy from Crushing Debt and Restore the American Dream: The U.S. people must make consumption sacrifices if they want to balance the country's budget. The U.S. must cap the home-mortgage interest deduction at $12,000 for individuals and $20,000 for joint-filing couples; gradually increase the Social Security retirement age to 68 between 1995 and 2006; raise federal taxes on cigarettes to $1.00 per pack and on alcoholic beverages to $16.00 per proof gallon; limit the current open-ended tax subsidy for employer-sponsored health care at the average cost of insurance coverage; phase in an increase in the federal gasoline tax of 50¢ per gallon between now and 2000; and implement a steeply progressive graduated entitlement-benefit reduction that would withhold a percentage of federal benefits from households with incomes above the U.S. median. These sacrifices would bring $202 billion.

**Big government reads its own obituary.** Howard Gleckman. *Business Week* 42–3 My 22 '95

On May 9–10, the Republican-controlled House and Senate Budget Committees presented fiscal agendas that not only propose to balance the budget but would profoundly restructure government. The Senate panel would eliminate over 100 programs and agencies, and the House would eliminate over 300. The GOP would ultimately eliminate many of the corporate subsidies that they created, as well as the social safety net constructed by the Democrats. Their ambitious plans will be under enormous pressure from Democrats and traditional Republican constituents, but even if the GOP fails to balance the budget by 2002, it has already won the debate over whether to substantially reduce government.

**MIT head warns federal cuts will decimate R&D.** Wil Lepkowski. *Chemical & Engineering News* 73:7 Jl 24 '95

United States research universities are upset over what they believe will be a 30 percent cut in federal research and development funding by the year 2002. The cuts would be part of Republican plans to balance the budget within the next seven years. Charles M. Vest, president of Massachusetts Institute of Technology, has joined an increasingly coordinated campaign by universities and their lobbyists to forestall the damage that they believe will take place if cuts are implemented. Speaking before the National Press Club, Vest said that America is in danger of disinvesting in its future and that the cost of drifting toward mediocrity in science, technology, and advanced education is too great to pay. Vest's views about the implications of federal policy changes are discussed.

**The Michigan experiment.** Peter Overby. *Common Cause Magazine* 20:11–6 Spr '94

Michigan governor John Engler is intent on de-inventing government. He has trimmed two departments, shuttered a third, frozen civil service pay, eliminated General Assistance (GA), and announced plans to contract out or sell other government operations. By eliminating GA, Engler kept his campaign promise not to raise taxes to balance the state budget, but incalculable costs were shifted to local hospitals, jails, and other facilities that service poor and homeless people. Engler got into a jam when he pledged to eliminate local property taxes that funded schools and allowed the legislature to slash the taxes before finding replacement revenues. In order to come up with the funds, he agreed to raise other taxes, including the sales or income tax, thereby alienating certain anti-tax factions. Voters will pass judgment on how to finance the schools in a March 15 [1994] referendum. The role of the Mackinac Center in Michigan's policies is discussed.

**Balanced budget baloney.** Malcolm S. Forbes, Jr.. *Forbes* 153:28 Ap 11 '94

Fortunately, the Senate has again narrowly defeated a balanced budget amendment to the Constitution. There are several reasons why such an amendment is a bad idea: Unlike states, most of which must balance budgets for current expenses and finance capital budgets by debt, Washington makes no distinction between money spent on capital projects or current expenses; there are other pressing problems in government finance; a balanced budget amendment without a line-veto provision would not allow the president to cut specific parts of an appropriations bill without vetoing the entire package; major tax and spending decisions could ultimately be made by federal judges; and Congress still uses "static analysis" to estimate tax receipts, a method that encourages tax increases instead of job-creating tax cuts. Until these matters are dealt with, the balanced budget amendment deserves to go nowhere.

**The looming budget battle over Medicare.** Ann Reilly Dowd. *Fortune* 131:20 My 29 '95

Republicans in Congress are proposing major cuts in Medicare as part of their strategy to balance the federal budget. They argue that Medicare may be bankrupt by the year 2002 unless spending growth is curbed. Specific steps will probably include more managed care, means testing, and payment cuts to providers. Congressional leaders plan to attach these controversial measures to bills that President Clinton must sign, such as those affecting the debt ceiling. The American Association of Retired Persons and the medical community are organizing and raising funds to oppose the Republican initiatives, but GOP strategists insist that they are not worried.

**Flat tax: a real bargain: would free up more dollars for home buyers.** Michael K. Evans. *IW: The Management Magazine* 244:86 S 4 '95

Studies funded by the National Association of Realtors erroneously conclude that a flat tax and the accompanying elimination of the mortgage deduction would hurt the housing market. In fact, a flat tax would balance the budget in five years, causing mortgage rates to drop approximately 2½ percent. Lower mortgage rates would spur home sales. In addition, because homeowners, on average, have higher income than renters, their tax bill would diminish, causing their after-tax income to rise rather than stay the same.

**Three blacks could lose Cabinet posts if GOP budget cut plan is passed in Congress.** *Jet* 88:6+ My 29 '95

Three of the four Black members of President Clinton's cabinet may lose their jobs if their departments are eliminated under proposed Republican budget cuts. The Republican-dominated Congress wants to balance the budget by 2002 and is seeking $1.4 trillion in savings. Already targeted for phaseout are the departments of Commerce (headed by Ron Brown), Energy (headed by Hazel O'Leary), and Veterans' Affairs (headed by Jesse Brown). The proposal, made last November when the GOP gained control of Congress, has stirred a hornet's nest of opposition and will probably lead to a year-long, race-tinged power struggle on Capitol Hill.

**Hollowgramm.** Robert Wright. *The New Republic* 212:4 Ap 3 '95

The closer Phil Gramm gets to real power, the more closely he resembles a generic Washington politician. Like most politicians, the conservative Gramm is afraid to attack the middle-class entitlements that consume a big portion of the federal budget. During a recent appearance on "Meet the Press," he vowed that he'd never touch Social Security to help balance the budget and emphatically denied that he'd raise the Medicare deductible. Gramm did call for cuts in welfare, but that will accomplish little because welfare is such a small portion of the budget. Moreover, it is hardly courageous to demand sacrifice from welfare recipients, who were never going to vote for him anyway. Even more outrageous is his claim that trying to balance the budget on the backs of poor people will save the underclass, a lie that is offensive even by Washington standards.

**Simon's simple pie.** *The New Yorker* 70:6+ F 28 '94

Illinois Democratic senator Paul Simon has proposed a Constitutional amendment to balance the federal budget that would virtually outlaw social reform if it were enacted. The amendment requires that total outlays for any fiscal year not exceed total receipts, unless three-fifths of each House of Congress provides by law for a specific excess of outlays by a rollcall vote. The amendment would frustrate President Clinton's plans for public investment, enshrine an economic dogma that would cripple a pragmatic response to changing conditions, and deprive families and businesses of federal resources. Congress would be faced with ruinous cuts in public investments, education, infrastructure, defense, and entitlements; having no alternative, it would presumably raise taxes. Perhaps the most harmful consequence of this amendment is that it casts into doubt the legitimacy of majority rule.

**Clinton's statement on plan to balance federal budget by 2005.** Bill Clinton. *New York Times* A18 Je 14 '95

The text of last night's televised address by President Clinton, in which he discusses his plan to balance the Federal budget within the next ten years, is presented.

## Round 1 on Republican budget begins in Senate committee.
David E. Rosenbaum. *New York Times* A24 My 9 '95

In a Senate Budget Committee meeting devoted to opening speeches, Republicans and Democrats staked out political positions for the days of debate that lie ahead. Republicans maintained that the country's economic future rests on their plan to balance the Federal budget over the next seven years. Democrats countered that the Republicans are more interested in protecting the privileged at the expense of the poor and aged than they are in advocating fiscal discipline.

## Senate panel offers budget that balances. David E. Rosenbaum.
*New York Times* A1+ My 10 '95

Republican senators today proposed a historic plan to balance the federal budget with cuts in projected Government spending of nearly a trillion dollars over the next seven years. Although the plan demonstrates in actual dollars and cents how the Republicans intend to reach this goal, it is in many respects short on details.

## House panel homes in on NIH. Andrew Lawler & Jeffrey Mervis. *Science* 267:1759 Mr 24 '95

Biomedical researchers have been shocked by the House Budget Committee's proposals for slashing $190 billion in federal spending over the next five years to pay for the tax cuts promised by the House Republicans' "Contract With America." The most significant threat to research within the committee's budget package is a proposed 5 percent cut in the National Institutes of Health's budget for 1996, to be followed by a spending freeze for the rest of the decade. The package also calls for cuts in NASA, the Department of Energy, the National Oceanic and Atmospheric Administration, and the Interior Department. Budget Committee Chair Representative John Kasich (R-OH) asserts that even deeper cuts will be detailed in May, when the committee is due to submit a plan to pay for its tax cuts and balance the federal budget by 2002.

## NASA mission gets down to earth. Andrew Lawler. *Science* 269:1208–10 S 1 '95

The National Aeronautics and Space Administration (NASA) is revising its plans for the multibillion-dollar Earth Observing System (EOS). The EOS program will involve investigations by thousands of researchers into the interaction of the land, sea, and atmosphere and the impact of human activity on the environment. The effort lacks solid support from the scientific community, and it is disliked by House Republicans because of its expense and its environmental focus. To counter criticisms of the program, NASA managers intend to shift the balance of the EOS away from long-term global change and toward acquiring information that will be immediately useful to such groups as farmers and the fishing industry. The degree to which they succeed will become evident in the coming weeks, when the National Academy of Science releases a report on the program's status and Congress determines the program's 1996 budget.

## Tearing into the deficit. George J. Church. *Time* 145:30–4 My 22 '95

A cover story looks at the latest Republican proposals to balance the federal budget. Republicans in Congress have sponsored resolutions that would reduce the federal deficit to zero by fiscal year 2002. Expenditures would be reduced by $1.4 trillion over the next seven years, and 284 federal agencies and programs would be eliminated. The House and Senate Budget Committees have approved these resolutions, and both chambers will probably vote to adopt them this week. Both houses must later consider actual appropriations, and eventually a reconciliation bill must receive President Clinton's signature or win passage over his veto. Even in the preliminary budget resolutions, House and Senate Republicans differ on tax cuts and defense spending. Democrats have denounced the proposals as an attempt to finance a tax cut for wealthy Americans at the expense of the elderly and unfortunate.

## We can still balance the budget. Paul W. McCracken. *Wall Street Journal* A14 Mr 6 '95

For the federal budget to be brought into basic balance by the target year of 2002, the government must commit to a limit to total spending before it sets its budget. When budgetary components are considered on an item-by-item basis, the resulting budget is always too large. In this vein, the Republican party should try again to garner passage of the balanced budget amendment. The measure could do in this era what the balanced budget tradition did so effectively for the country from its birth until the Great Depression.

## Allies against deficit split over plan to amend constitution to require balanced federal budget. Paulette Thomas. *Wall Street Journal* A20 F 24 '94

Although Washington deficit hawks Carol Cox Wait and Martha Phillips have a lot in common, they currently find themselves in sharp opposition to one another as Congress again takes up a proposal for a constitutional amendment that would require a balanced federal budget. Phillips, executive director of the Concord Coalition, believes that a constitutional amendment is the only hope for the U.S. to unburden itself of interest payments that total $213 billion this year alone. In contrast, Wait, president of the Committee for a Responsible Federal Budget, thinks that changing the Constitution is a prescription for disaster. Instead of voting for an amendment, Wait believes that lawmakers should make the hard choices now about how to balance the federal budget.

## The perils of Pauline—again. Mortimer B. Zuckerman. *U.S. News & World Report* 119:104 S 25 '95

Any deal between the two factions of government regarding the budget and tax agenda needs to show a commitment to reducing the deficit. President Clinton feels that the Republicans' budget proposals contain deeper cuts than are needed and that tax cuts would disproportionately benefit the well-to-do. He is likely to veto a reconciliation bill, without which the budget and tax agenda cannot be rescued. The president must acknowledge his endorsement of the notion of a tax cut, the need to cut the growth in spending on Medicare and Medicaid to avert the bankruptcy of both programs, and the need to balance the budget. Moreover, Clinton must show that he can work with the Republican Congress—a kind of proof to his reasoning that his reelection would moderately influence Republican zealotry.